LEVERAGE

—YOUR—

MINDSET

FOR GOLFERS

BREAKING MENTAL BARRIERS AND
ELEVATING YOUR GAME

RICKY KALMON

Published and distributed by:
SOUND WISDOM
P.O. Box 310
Shippensburg, PA 17257-0310
717-530-2122
info@soundwisdom.com

www.soundwisdom.com

ISBN 13 TP: 978-1-64095-585-1

ISBN 13 eBook: 978-1-64095-586-8

For Worldwide Distribution, Printed in the U.S.A.

1 2025

DISCLAIMER

It is very important that you understand that the techniques and/ or exercises in this book cannot make you do anything. Your willingness and openness create the momentum and direction you desire. Ricky Kalmon/Kalmon Productions, LLC motivational programs and techniques should not be considered a form of therapy or be used for the treatment of physical, emotional, or medical issues. If expert assistance or counseling is needed, the services of a competent medical professional should always be sought. Neither Ricky Kalmon nor Kalmon Productions, LLC shall be liable for any physical, psychological, emotional, financial, or commercial damages, including but not limited to special, incidental, consequential, or other damages. You are responsible for your own choices, actions, and results.

AUDIO SUPPORT PROGRAM

This book comes with an audio support program for each chapter. Download the Ricky Kalmon app by visiting **rickykalmon.com/app** or scanning the QR code below. You can also go to your app store and search the title RICKY KALMON. Once you download it and create an account, you will enter the app. Click on the program titled *Leverage Your Mindset Audio Support*. Then click on the program titled *For GOLFERS*. Use the password **RKCADDIE** to claim access to this content. This will unlock and give you access to the specific audio program designed for this book. After each chapter, there are instructions about which audio track to listen to. Please listen only to the track correlated with each day's activities and instructions.

*To my incredible wife and family who
have been my inspiration to be a better
version of myself every day!*

*And to my dear friends who inspired
me to write this book and help others
to succeed at the game they love.*

CONTENTS

MINDSET COACH

The game between your ears will
no longer be a challenge.

THE SIGNIFICANT GAP between where you play golf
today and where you could be playing golf lies on the course
between your ears. I am sure you have heard this before. Golf
is as much a mental game as it is a physical one. I am sure you
have said all too often that "My mind got the best of me." It is a
common reaction to a not-your-best game. Yet, we don't replace
our response with the right reset and redirect. We can become
so accustomed to relying on our physical abilities and focusing
on other areas of our lives—our careers, families, or fitness—that
we neglect the most critical aspect of our game: our mindset. The
pressures and distractions of daily life can clutter our thoughts,
slowing our ability to think clearly and strategically on the course.
Like fine-tuning your swing, your mind requires regular updates
and resets to operate fully. To truly excel in golf, you must sharpen
your mental *and* physical game.

I'm Ricky Kalmon, and I show people worldwide the power of thought and how to leverage their mindset. The words we say to ourselves and the mental images we focus on are the most effective tools we will ever know. I am a mindset expert, motivational speaker, and hypnotist. But don't let the term "hypnotist" lead you astray. I'm not talking about controlling thoughts or putting people into trances.

Hypnosis is simply about achieving a state of deep relaxation and using positive suggestions to create the changes you seek. This relaxed state enhances your mindfulness, allowing you to channel your intentions toward shaping your desired new reality. It's like updating the software on your computer or mobile device. In fact, all hypnosis is self-hypnosis, which I often refer to as "self-hypnosis meditation." You are entirely in control, guiding your thoughts and actions to bring about the changes you want.

Now, let me introduce you to the concept of becoming a "hypnotic golfer" as you break mental barriers and elevate your game.

This book is a 14-day plan. Read a chapter a day for the next 14 days. Invest 10-15 minutes daily to make mindset changes to train your brain. Every person has thoughts and beliefs that either motivate or limit their success. We convince ourselves that we cannot achieve a goal or do better, and those thoughts are programmed into our mindset. Then, before we even attempt to make progress, our mindset reminds us that it's not possible.

The opposite is also true. When we tell ourselves that we can do better or accomplish a goal, our mindset goes to work to motivate us and strengthen our desire and belief that the goals and results we want are within our reach. There is extraordinary potential lying dormant within your own mind. The key to unlocking that potential is personal awareness of your thoughts and beliefs. In the next 14 days, we will take that personal awareness journey together, and you will learn how to update your mind to work *with* you to improve your performance, achievements, and enjoyment of life.

You picked up this book for one reason: results. By completing this journey of self-awareness, you'll unlock those positive results on and off the golf course! This book is your guide to leveraging your mindset to enhance your mental game beyond technique. The strategies within these pages are designed, no matter your goal or desired outcome, if you commit that change is possible. They'll elevate your belief, engagement, and achievement in anything you pursue. What you learn here won't just apply to your golf game; it will spill over into your professional and personal life as well.

Do you want to be less stressed and more successful? To grow your business, stay focused, driven, appreciative, and healthy? To navigate changes with ease and take control of both your personal and professional life is the purpose of you engaging the concept and implantation of simple yet powerful techniques. I'm sure one or more of these aspirations caught your attention—perhaps all of them. We all have a deep desire to play our best round of golf and achieve success in other areas of life. So, what's holding you back from turning these hopes and dreams into reality? It's all about your mindset.

Mindset is a program running in your subconscious mind. You're already using your subconscious in everything you do.

Isn't it time to actively collaborate with it and harness its power to create the changes you desire? The process is simple and doesn't require much time or effort. There are no special skills needed. You already have all the tools—your only investment is the desire to make a change.

Over the next 14 days, you will learn how to surpass your own expectations. In just two short weeks, you'll discover your greatest caddie and ally—your mindset—and master the art of using it to dramatically improve your golf game and your life. When you harness your thoughts, you remove the limits on your potential and open yourself up to unlimited possibilities.

Life is too short not to enjoy playing the game you love. I am thrilled to be your mindset coach and offer you ways to IGNITE YOUR TALENT!

IMPORTANT: This book is set up as a 14-day plan. The first chapter (Day One) corresponds with the first day. Ideally, you should complete the chapters in order, starting with Day One. Then, complete one chapter each day until the program is finished.

If you have not already downloaded my app, please download it by visiting rickykalmon.com/app. You can also go to your app store and search the title RICKY KALMON. Once you download it and create an account, you will enter the app. Click on the program titled *Leverage Your Mindset Audio Support.* Then click on the program titled *For GOLFERS.* Use the password **RKCADDIE** to claim access to this content. This will unlock and give you access to the specific audio program designed for this book. After each chapter, there are instructions about which audio track to listen to. Please listen only to the track correlated with each day's activities and instructions.

HOW WE SABOTAGE OUR SUCCESS BEFORE WE START

Get out of your own way. Life's
too short to play bad golf!

GOLF IS BOTH a physical and mental game, but many golfers overlook how often the battle is won or lost in their mind, even before they swing a club. Think back to the times when you've stood over the ball and thought, *I better not hook this*, only to follow through and do exactly that. Then, as if to seal the outcome, you reaffirm the mistake with, *See, I told you so*. What just happened? You've programmed your mind to act on that last message of belief.

The power of your thoughts dictated the shot. There are also those moments of internal conversation where we overanalyze every detail of our swing or get caught up in endless "what if" scenarios—fearing how others will judge our performance. These self-imposed pressures can take us out of the present moment, shifting our focus from playing our best to worrying about external perceptions, which ultimately hinder our progress.

Leverage Your Mindset for Golfers isn't just about building confidence or overcoming limiting beliefs—it's about fully embracing the present moment. Whether it's a drive, chip, putt, or approach shot, it's about resetting your mind for every stroke. The more you learn to redirect your thoughts, the better you'll play. This will become an automatic unconscious programming. Yes, when you truly understand and learn how to implement the strategies, techniques, and philosophy of leveraging your mindset, it becomes an unconscious automatic programming.

Now, think of your brain as a computer. Your mindset is like the software that runs it. If the software isn't up to date, the system lags. Sometimes, malware (self-doubt, fear, negative thoughts) slows you down. Like those updates you ignore on your phone, your mind needs an upgrade today. Click the "install now" button on your mental game, because every part of your success hinges on how you manage your thoughts.

Update Your Internal Software

Updating your internal software—your mindset—allows you to focus on what truly matters in the game. You'll find success not only through practice but through a sharp, resilient mindset. Whether you're a weekend golfer or aspiring pro, your mental game must be in peak form.

I've worked with top performers in various fields: NFL and MLB athletes, Fortune 500 CEOs, and, yes, elite golfers. Every one of them spends years on physical training. Yet all too often, reducing stress and building mental resilience take little priority. We all know that mindset is critical to success, yet we often neglect to invest in ourselves the time needed to train our brain. Here's the reality;if you don't make time to prioritize your mindset now, it will cost you later. Whether it's lost focus on the course, missed opportunities, or mental fatigue, failing to update your mind will always come at a price. Even if you are already successful, can you take yourself to the next level? Yes, so don't put off what you should be doing today.

My philosophy is about you investing in yourself. We set time on our calendars to show up for meetings and events. We are expected to be on time and the invite holds us accountable for appointments. But when was the last time you set a calendar invite just for yourself—to reset, refocus, and redirect your energy? Yes, I am saying for you to show up for yourself. Taking time to reduce stress and cultivate calmness and clarity is essential for improving your mental game of golf.

Take time to reduce stress and cultivate calmness and clarity to improve your mental game of golf.

By dedicating intentional time to this practice, you're giving yourself permission to prioritize your mental well-being and strengthen the clarity you bring to the course. Start by scheduling time for you—time to invest in your mindset and watch how it transforms your game and your life.

Prioritize Yourself

At the end of this chapter, take a moment to prioritize yourself. Set a calendar meeting with just you—10 minutes to be aware, present, and to reset your mind. Use this time to redirect your energy and focus on creating calmness and clarity. This simple act of scheduling intentional time for yourself can be a game-changer for your mental game of golf, helping you approach each day and each round with a clearer, more focused mindset.

Each chapter will ask you to dedicate time to this mindset reboot. We will add elements of breathing, meditation, guided thought, and mindset updates. Start now, and make it a habit that continues to elevate your performance both on and off the course.

You may not realize it yet, but your mindset might be running on your old autopilot system and it could be dulling your edge. To sharpen your game—both mentally and physically—you must continually update your mental software. The stakes are higher than you think. Just like you'd protect and nurture any valuable investment, treat your mindset with the same care. Starting today, allow yourself the time to recalibrate. Treat your mindset like a complex, multimillion-dollar portfolio. Give it the attention it deserves, maintain it, and watch the results multiply in your game and life.

This journey is about reprogramming your mind to embrace success and crush the self-doubt that holds you back. Our thoughts are like automatic programs running in the background—what I call AutoThoughts. These are the repetitive messages that shape how we perform. For example, when you ask yourself, "Can I be more successful?" Destructive AutoThoughts may whisper back, "Not today. This is too difficult. Change is hard." Meanwhile, constructive AutoThoughts affirm your potential: "Yes, I can. I've got this. I'm talented, I'm worthy."

It's not enough to simply think positively. You must take deliberate action to create constructive AutoThoughts that empower you to succeed. These thoughts will become your driving force, influencing how you feel, perform, and even how others perceive you. Identifying destructive AutoThoughts starts by recognizing those negative, limiting beliefs that creep into your mind. When you hear them—like doubts about your ability to make a shot or frustration about past mistakes—acknowledge them as destructive AutoThoughts. Then, actively replace them with constructive AutoThoughts. I will dive deeper into AutoThoughts in Day Three. This simple concept is the core and root of our mindset.

Consciously Reframe Your Thoughts

By taking conscious steps to reframe your thoughts, you'll slowly shift your mental programming to favor success over failure, empowerment over self-doubt. Much like a computer, your mind needs regular maintenance to keep running at its best. Every successful golfer knows that winning requires constant mental updates. Today is the day you install those updates and unleash your full potential.

The truth is, your brain thrives on stimulation—it's the control center of your entire body. Feed it the right energy and you'll operate at your highest level. Don't wait for tomorrow or the next round. Begin today by committing to Leverage Your Mindset as an "AMAZING GOLFER," and watch how the course of your game—and your life—transforms.

Can you be a better player today and a better version of yourself? YES! Who is really holding you back from reaching your daily potential? The answer, more often than not, is YOU. The thoughts you allow to take root and the words you speak—whether to yourself or others—shape your reality. What we say and think matters because our language and internal dialogue have transformative power, not only for us but also for those who hear it.

Positive or negative, the words we use create the blueprint for our actions and outcomes. It's time to get out of your own way and stop letting limiting beliefs sabotage your progress. Embrace the power of your words, thoughts, and actions. It's time to strive to be a better player daily and a better version of you.

"Embrace the power of your words, thoughts, and actions.

Mindsetcaddie Reset Introduction

I'd like to introduce two key elements that will accompany each chapter, each day. The *MindsetCaddie Reset* serves as a summary of the main concepts of each chapter, but it goes beyond just a recap. This element is designed to reinforce positive thoughts and insights, allowing you to internalize the lessons and integrate them into your mindset.

Just as pro golfers rely on caddies for support, strategy, and guidance, your mindset can serve as your most valuable caddie. Caddies help golfers navigate the course, provide strategic advice, and offer emotional support, enabling them to perform at their best. Throughout this book, my goal is to show you how your mindset can fulfill that same role—enhancing your focus, boosting your confidence, and guiding your decisions on the course.

Each Reset will encourage reflection and application, guiding you to actively engage with the material. This not only helps solidify your understanding but also empowers you to cultivate a stronger mental game. By reflecting on your experiences and setting intentions, you can turn insights into actionable strategies that enhance your performance.

Moreover, these resets provide practical exercises and prompts to keep you focused and motivated. By regularly engaging with the MindsetCaddie Reset, you can transform knowledge into lasting habits, fostering resilience, confidence, and a more empowered approach to your golf journey. Embrace these opportunities for growth, and watch as your mindset elevates your game to new heights, just like a trusted caddie would.

MindsetCaddie Redirect Introduction

The MindsetCaddie Redirect is an essential component designed to provide you with actionable exercises that help you implement and engrave the concepts from each chapter. These exercises are tailored to reinforce your learning, ensuring that the insights you gain become an integral part of your mental game.

Each Redirect guides you through practical activities that encourage active participation and reflection, helping you to apply what you've learned in real-world scenarios. Whether it's visualization techniques, mindfulness practices, or strategic goal-setting, these exercises will challenge you to think critically and creatively about your approach to golf.

As you progress through the book, the MindsetCaddie Redirect will build upon previous chapters, deepening your understanding and enhancing your skills. Each exercise is designed to connect the dots between concepts, fostering a cohesive and holistic mindset transformation. By consistently engaging with these redirects, you will cultivate habits that reinforce resilience, boost confidence, and empower you to tackle challenges with a renewed perspective.

Think of the MindsetCaddie Redirect as your personal toolkit, equipping you with the resources you need to navigate the course of your mental journey. By embracing these actionable exercises, you'll not only enhance your performance on the golf course but also develop a stronger, more resilient mindset that supports your overall growth and success.

"Cultivate habits that reinforce resilience, boost confidence, and empower you to tackle challenges with a renewed perspective.

As you dedicate more time to invest in your game and yourself, treat this time with seriousness and intention. Recognize that every moment you spend honing your skills and nurturing your mindset is an opportunity for growth. Use this time to reflect on your goals, develop your techniques, and cultivate a positive mental attitude. Embrace the process, stay focused, and commit to making the most of this investment, knowing that it will pay off both on and off the course. Your journey toward improvement starts with the choices you make now, so approach each practice session and reflection with purpose and determination.

As you complete this chapter, wrapping up Day One, remember that this book is intentionally designed with daily activities and actionable steps. While it might be tempting to power through the entire book in one sitting, true growth and meaningful change come from consistent practice and reflection. Give yourself the space and time to absorb, apply, and internalize these lessons. By taking it one day at a time, you allow each step to build upon the last, creating a lasting transformation in your mindset and approach. The real impact lies not in how quickly you finish, but in how deeply you embrace each concept and make it part of your daily life. Trust the process, commit to the journey, and watch how small, consistent actions lead to profound results over time.

MindsetCaddie Reset

> **The Power of Thought in Golf:** Your thoughts directly influence your performance on the course. When you focus on negative outcomes *(I better not hook this),* you often reinforce those thoughts, causing the exact outcome you were trying to avoid. Reprogramming your mind with positive, constructive thoughts can reshape your game.

> **Mindset as Software:** Your mindset operates like software that needs constant updates to function optimally. Neglecting mental updates, such as eliminating self-doubt and building resilience, leads to sluggish performance, both on the course and in life.

> **AutoThoughts Management:** Destructive AutoThoughts are negative, automatic beliefs that undermine success. Recognizing and replacing these with constructive AutoThoughts—positive affirmations about your potential—empowers you to shift from self-doubt to self-belief, influencing not only your performance but also how others perceive you.

MindsetCaddie Redirect

> Set a calendar reminder for 10 minutes each day, and make it a non-negotiable part of your routine. The time can change if necessary—what truly matters is your commitment to showing up for yourself every day. Even if you have to move your daily reminder around, just make sure you do it. There's no excuse not to dedicate this small window of time to refocus your mindset and elevate your mental well-being. Think of this as an investment in your most valuable asset—yourself. These 10 minutes are not a luxury, but a necessity for your

growth and mental clarity. Stay consistent, and you'll begin to see how such a simple practice can create a ripple effect, strengthening your mindset and positively influencing all areas of your life.

> During this personal time, become fully conscious of your inner voice. Ask yourself: *Is it building me up or tearing me down?* Conduct a personal audit of your internal dialogue without judgment—just observe. Don't overthink this exercise; the goal is to notice. For the next 10 minutes, focus on redirecting any unhelpful thoughts. Turn off all distractions, find a quiet place, and simply sit in stillness. Pay attention to your breath— inhale deeply, exhale slowly. As you do, feel the rhythm of your breath and let it ground you in the present moment. Allow your thoughts to come and go, without attaching to them. Just be present and breathe. If your mind wanders, gently guide it back to your breath. This simple act of awareness is powerful. Use this time to reconnect with yourself and practice quieting the mental chatter that often clouds your mindset.

> The more you commit to this practice personal time, the more you will become aware of the power of your inner voice and learn to guide it toward constructive, positive thinking. We revisit this personal reflection time in the next chapter, Day Two, introducing new tools and techniques to enhance your mindset, including strategies for building resilience in the days to come.

> As an additional reinforcement tool, you can now listen to the Day One audio in the support program available on my app. This audio program is designed to complement and strengthen each day's lessons, helping you internalize the material more effectively. By integrating this tool into your daily routine, you gain deeper insights and accelerate your progress. My goal is to provide you with every resource needed to maximize your experience and achieve lasting transformation.

SELF-HYPNOSIS MEDITATION: NOT A SOFT SKILL, BUT A HARD SKILL

Control your thoughts,
control your outcomes.

WHEN WE THINK OF HYPNOSIS, many people might associate it with being a mysterious practice. Some categorize hypnosis and meditation as a soft skill. The truth is that it's a hard skill—grounded in science and the incredible capacity of the mind. Like mindfulness, hypnosis has profound effects on cognitive functions, influencing perception, focus, and reducing stress. Hypnosis is not a technique of snapping your fingers to create change. It requires consistent practice and engagement. Once mastered, hypnosis and mindfulness become powerful tools for high performers, especially golfers, where mental clarity is just as essential as physical technique.

Hypnosis and Mindfulness

Understanding how hypnosis works on the brain reveals why it's crucial to harness your mental state. Hypnosis and meditation are closely connected, both focusing on enhancing mental attention, reducing distractions, and promoting relaxation. I often remark that all hypnosis is self-hypnosis. In addition, meditation, and hypnosis overlap in execution and outcomes. In fact, my philosophy combines the two principles to *Self-Hypnosis Meditation.* This powerful tool can sharpen the mind and reduce stress, making these mental techniques invaluable for improving performance in both everyday life and on the golf course.

Look at it this way: a hypnotist does not put somebody in a "state of mind." The individual does. This is no different from a coach teaching an athlete. The hypnotist is merely the catalyst to helping the person visualize and get into a state of awareness; but in reality, individuals hypnotize themselves. Hypnosis is not being asleep or being unconscious. It's not being in an altered state. *Hypnosis* is a state of focused clarity, achieved through intentional breathing that calms the mind and directs attention toward a desired outcome.

You are never in a trance or unaware of what's going on. This is one of the biggest misconceptions of hypnosis. Nor are you being controlled by hypnosis itself. This powerful state of mind is nothing more than a tool for you to become more present and engaging when directing yourself toward your positive intentions. Self-hypnosis offers more than just a sense of calm—it's a powerful tool to help you relax, break unwanted habits, and reshape unhelpful thought patterns. In my experience, I have described this as a way to focus effort and influence your outcomes. .

Hypnosis is a state of focused clarity, achieved through intentional breathing that calms the mind and directs attention toward a desired outcome.

This isn't magic—it's the power of deliberate mental conditioning. I am often asked, "Who can be hypnotized?" and my response is, "Everyone." The process is simple so don't over-complicate it. At its core, hypnosis operates by shifting attention and perception in the brain.

According to an article in *healthline.com*, dated August 17, 2021, Dr. David Spiegel, Stanford psychiatrist and expert in the field of hypnosis, explains that mental rehearsal has as much effect on athletic performance as physical rehearsal. He describes self-hypnosis as a process of focusing and disconnecting from expectations and worries, allowing you to be present and to perform your best. He states, "It's not something that someone does to you. It's something you help your brain do to yourself."

Research shows that hypnosis heightens focus while reducing self-consciousness, allowing the mind to be more receptive to positive changes. It's like pressing a mental reset button, breaking free from unhelpful patterns and making way for better outcomes.

Similarly, *mindfulness* helps you stay anchored in the present, regulating stress, sharpening focus, and avoiding the mental pitfalls that lead to self-doubt or distraction. It creates lasting changes in how the brain processes information, affecting the areas responsible for emotional regulation, attention, and decision-making. Both hypnosis and mindfulness revolve around "focused attention."

This is what separates top performers from the rest. Mastering the ability to lock into the present moment provides clarity and enhances performance by shutting out distractions. In golf, this can mean the difference between sinking a perfect putt or letting stress cloud your judgment and missing an easy shot. The power of focused attention allows you to perform optimally by immersing yourself in the moment.

Mindset Conditioning

The ability to snap into this state of focus is a skill that requires deliberate practice. Imagine standing at the tee, with the people around you, the wind, and even your past performance fading into the background as you concentrate solely on the shot in front of you. That's the synergy of mindset conditioning—keeping your attention sharp and grounded in the present moment. But this isn't just a mental exercise; it's a trainable skill with measurable outcomes.

Mindset conditioning is often misunderstood as a soft skill due to its association with emotional awareness and calmness. However, it requires the same level of discipline, structured learning, and repeated application that define hard skills such as improving your golf swing through practice and technique. Mastering mindset conditioning demands regular, focused training. Through deliberate repetition, you refine your ability to enter this focused state at will, just as you would refine a physical technique in your game.

When you step back and look at people you admire because of their mental toughness and fortitude, that is mindset. Their ability to stay calm under pressure, adapt to challenges, and maintain focus is not a coincidence—it's the result of consistent mindset conditioning.

The benefits of mindset conditioning can be quantified. Studies have shown that regular mental training leads to observable changes in brain function, particularly in areas responsible for focus, emotional regulation, and stress response. The ability to control your mental state and maintain composure under pressure is not a vague or abstract skill—it is a concrete ability that can be honed and measured over time.

This ability goes beyond just mental calmness—it's a performance enhancer. Athletes, corporate professionals, and high performers have adopted mindset conditioning as a tool to sharpen focus, reduce errors, and improve results. The effectiveness of these techniques can be evaluated through metrics such as improved performance consistency, reduced stress levels, and better decision-making. This is why mindset conditioning is increasingly being taught with structured techniques in coaching programs, not as optional emotional tools but as core components that directly impact outcomes.

"The ability to control your mental state goes beyond mental calmness—it's a performance enhancer.

The hard skill of mindset conditioning, when applied consistently, integrates seamlessly into your performance and present state of mind. It becomes an automatic, almost mechanical part of your routine, giving you an edge over your competition—not just mentally but in terms of results.

Your mindset influences every swing, every decision, and how you react to both stress and success. When you harness the power of mental conditioning—enhanced through self-hypnosis meditation and mindfulness—your mindset becomes your greatest asset. It guides you through challenges, keeps you present, and amplifies your ability to perform under pressure. Your thoughts won't be clouded by past mistakes or future worries; instead, you will remain focused and grounded in the moment, fully engaged in the task at hand—or club in hand.

Obstacles

The real question becomes, are *you* the obstacle standing in the way of your success? Many people don't recognize how much their mindset determines their ability to reduce stress, stay focused, and perform at their best. The truth is, your mind can either be your greatest ally or your biggest barrier—it's up to you to decide.

So much of our daily lives is done without thinking. Typing on a keyboard is a perfect example of an unconscious behavior that becomes automatic through repetition and practice. When someone first learns to type, they must consciously think about the location of each key, how to position their fingers, and ensure the right letters are pressed. This requires deliberate attention and can feel slow and cumbersome.

However, as a person practices typing regularly, their brain and muscles adapt. This process, known as muscle memory, allows the fingers to automatically "remember" where each key is located. Over time, the conscious effort fades, and the action of typing becomes smooth and instinctive. The brain no longer has to focus on the mechanics of finding each key. Instead, attention shifts entirely to the thoughts or words being communicated, freeing up cognitive resources for creativity, problem-solving, or organizing ideas.

An example of learned unconscious *bad* behavior is interrupting others during conversations. Initially, someone might interrupt because they are eager to share their thoughts or feel strongly about the topic at hand. However, over time, this can become an ingrained habit, occurring automatically without conscious awareness. As this behavior repeats, the person may interrupt others without realizing it, driven by an unconscious need to be heard or contribute. This habit can be harmful to relationships and communication, as it can make others feel disrespected or unheard. Even though the person may not intend to be rude, the behavior has become automatic and unconscious, reflecting *a lack of mindful listening.*

Breaking this habit often requires self-awareness and active effort to pause and listen before speaking, retraining the mind to be more considerate in conversations. This kind of unconscious behavior demonstrates how the brain optimizes repetitive tasks. Once learned, the task becomes automatic, requiring little to no conscious thought. In fact, experienced typists can often type out entire paragraphs while engaging in other forms of thinking or conversation because the mechanical process is so deeply ingrained.

This phenomenon is a powerful illustration of how habits and skills, once mastered, can be executed effortlessly, allowing for multitasking or deeper focus on higher-level thinking. By mastering the hard skills of hypnosis and mindfulness, you gain control over your mental state, enabling you to focus your attention and enhance performance in all areas of life—whether on the golf course, in the office, or in personal relationships. These skills are not luxuries, they are essentials. And once they are part of your routine, the results will far exceed your expectations.

Remember, *life is full of opportunities, but it's your mental state that determines how well you seize them.* Your thoughts shape your reality; and by developing the hard skill of focused attention, you will leverage your mindset that will unlock the potential to reduce stress, enhance performance, and achieve more than you ever thought possible.

I have your attention now, don't I? Of course I do. Let's continue this journey by implementing this hard skill of transformation and empowerment.

Mindsetcaddie Reset

> **Powerful Tools for High Performers:** Hypnosis and mindfulness are techniques that enhance mental clarity, focus, and stress management, making them indispensable tools for achieving peak performance in any area of life.

> **Impact Outcomes:** Hypnosis is not about losing control—it is about mastering your mental state, allowing you to shift your attention and perception to unlock greater personal and professional growth.

❯ **Mindset Conditioning:** Mastering these mental techniques empowers you to break through distractions, remain grounded under pressure, and elevate your performance in everything from sports to business.

Mindsetcaddie Redirect

❯ Commit to a Daily 10-Minute Mental Reset: Continue your practice of spending 10 minutes each day to reset and redirect your thoughts. Use this time to acknowledge any distractions or negative thoughts and consciously shift your focus to your goals and positive intentions. Visualize success and engage your mind in constructive thinking.

❯ Begin by finding a quiet, comfortable space where you can sit without distractions. Close your eyes and take a deep breath in, feeling the air fill your lungs. Slowly exhale, letting go of any tension or stress. Focus your attention on your breathing, noticing the natural rhythm of each inhale and exhale. Breathe effortlessly, without trying to control it. During this time, simply embrace the ease of your breath and the sense of inner peace it brings. Take full advantage of doing nothing but being present in the moment, allowing yourself to just be. As you sit in stillness, allow your thoughts to come and go without judgment. If your mind wanders, gently bring your focus back to your breath. Feel the rise and fall of your chest or the sensation of air passing through your nostrils. Stay present with this simple act of breathing. Let yourself enjoy the present moment.

> As an additional reinforcement tool, you can now listen to Day Two in the audio program available on my app. I will guide you through a breathing and meditation exercise to promote calmness, awareness, and guided thought.

GOLF AUTOTHOUGHTS™ AND THE ROLE OF EMOTIONAL INTELLIGENCE

Embrace a deliberate mindset,
where determination becomes
the architect of your reality!

YOU'RE WALKING into the clubhouse, and someone passes by you. Without thinking, you look up and smile, perhaps making a small gesture. This was an unconscious reaction, an automatic response that happens without deliberate thought. In that brief moment, your smile can instantly improve both your mood and the other person's, strengthening the connection between you. This is a reflection of your brain's association between that person and feelings of happiness or comfort.

Now consider a different scenario: Have you ever reacted with frustration or anger when stuck in traffic? This is a common negative unconscious response. Without consciously thinking, you may tense up, sigh, or even yell, allowing the stress of the situation to take over. This reaction doesn't solve the problem and can actually escalate your stress levels, affecting your mood and overall well-being for the rest of the day. This automatic negative response is often the result of ingrained patterns related to stress or feeling a lack of control.

Emotional Intelligence

In both examples, your reactions and actions were a result of your emotional intelligence. *By developing emotional intelligence, we can harness our unconscious reactions to work in our favor.* Emotional intelligence enables us to be more aware of our positive automatic responses, such as smiling, and intentionally use them to build stronger connections and foster positive environments. For example, recognizing the power of a simple smile can help us be more mindful of creating warmth and trust in our interactions, even when we aren't consciously thinking about it.

On the other hand, emotional intelligence gives us the tools to manage and redirect negative unconscious reactions. Being aware of automatic negative responses, like frustration or anger in traffic, allows us to pause, assess the situation, and choose a more constructive reaction. Instead of letting stress escalate, we can use strategies such as deep breathing or reframing the situation to maintain calm and control. By doing so, we reduce the impact of negative emotions and create space for more positive outcomes, both for ourselves and those around us.

In essence, emotional intelligence helps us turn both positive and negative unconscious reactions into opportunities for growth, improved relationships, and enhanced emotional resilience.

Emotional intelligence (EI) is the ability to recognize, understand, and manage our own emotions while also being in tune with the emotions of others. As a golfer, EI plays a critical role in how you respond to the inevitable challenges of the game—whether it's recovering from a bad shot, handling the pressure of a crucial putt, or maintaining composure during a tense moment.

AutoThoughts™

At the core of my philosophy is a concept I introduced earlier: AutoThoughts. These are automatic, habitual thought patterns that influence how we perceive and respond to situations. In this chapter, we take a deep dive into the role of emotional intelligence in not only becoming aware of these AutoThoughts, but also learning how to harness them constructively.

> How do you react and respond under pressure?

> How aware are you of being unaware?

> How unaware are you of being unaware?

We often function on autopilot, repeating reactions, patterns, and habits without conscious awareness. Think about times when someone close to you pointed out a habit you weren't aware of, like slouching in a chair or poor table manners. You might respond defensively, acknowledging the habit but doing nothing to change it. If we were truly aware of these habits, would we still do them? Those around us often have a front-row seat to behaviors we overlook, but how often do we sit in the audience of our own lives and observe the outdated habits we wish to change?

Destructive AutoThoughts™

Unwanted destructive AutoThoughts are the automatic thoughts and responses rooted in fear, doubt, worry, and negativity. These thoughts impede your ability to stay present and perform optimally. However, by acknowledging that you own these thoughts, you can start to challenge and reshape them into more empowering narratives. This intentional rewiring of your mind not only fosters personal growth but also strengthens your trust in yourself, your swing, and your talent.

Identify and challenge negative thoughts: Start by paying close attention to your mental dialogue and recognize when destructive AutoThoughts arise. When you find yourself stuck in a loop of negativity, pause and question the validity of those thoughts. Is there real evidence supporting them, or are they simply assumptions or fears? Challenge these negative thoughts by seeking alternative perspectives and reframing them in a more positive and realistic light.

This practice is invaluable for transforming your thought patterns and mindset. By identifying and challenging negative thoughts, you break free from the cycle of self-limiting beliefs and open yourself to more positive and empowering perspectives. Over time, *you'll gain greater self-awareness and control over your mental responses, enabling you to reframe challenges as opportunities and adopt a growth-oriented mindset.*

Through this process, you will develop a greater understanding of how your thoughts influence your emotions, behaviors, and overall well-being. By continuously challenging negative thoughts and replacing them with more constructive ones, you create a mental environment conducive to being fully present and performing as your best self on the golf course.

Most of us react to and act upon our internal beliefs and thoughts, often without fully understanding how profoundly they shape our reality. We rarely stop to assess the internal operating system that runs beneath our conscious awareness, influencing our decisions, behaviors, and ultimately our results on and off the course.

This shift in perspective is often overlooked by our internal AutoThoughts. On the range, you're in a controlled environment where repetition builds confidence, but once on the course, your destructive AutoThoughts can creep in, focusing on fear of failure or past mistakes rather than adapting to new challenges. These thoughts create a disconnect between your preparation and performance. Recognizing and reshaping these AutoThoughts to be more constructive allows you to approach each shot with a clear, focused mindset, embracing change and seizing opportunities as they arise. This mental flexibility is what separates a good range session from great course performance.

"Consciously programming your thoughts unlocks the ability to shift your mindset, manage stress, and perform at a higher potential.

My goal is to show you how to take control of that system by becoming the lead programmer of your constructive Auto Thoughts—the automatic, empowering thoughts that set the tone for your mental and physical game. When you consciously program these thoughts, you unlock the ability to shift your mindset, manage stress, and perform at your highest potential. This approach will allow you to build a powerful, focused reality that strengthens both your mental resilience and physical precision as a golfer.

Emotional intelligence plays a pivotal role in this entire process. Through the lens of emotional intelligence, you become more aware of your AutoThoughts and their impact on your mental state and performance. High EI allows you to better manage frustration, remain composed after setbacks, and respond thoughtfully under pressure, rather than reacting impulsively. By honing your emotional intelligence, you not only gain mastery over your emotions but also over your mind's internal dialogue. This heightened awareness enables you to navigate the emotional highs and lows of the game, turning challenges into opportunities for growth and resilience.

Constructive AutoThoughts™

In addition, emotional intelligence fosters a deeper connection between your thoughts and physical execution on the course. By understanding the emotional triggers that spark destructive AutoThoughts and learning to shift them into constructive AutoThoughts, you can enhance your focus, control anxiety, and optimize your performance. Ultimately, emotional intelligence allows you to approach the game with confidence, poise, and mental clarity—traits that define elite golfers.

This book and process are designed to teach you how to update your internal operating system—the core set of beliefs, habits, and automatic thought patterns that shape how you approach the game of golf and life itself. Just like updating software improves performance, learning how to reprogram your mind through constructive AutoThoughts will enhance your mental agility, resilience, and focus. You will discover how to identify outdated, limiting thoughts and replace them with empowering ones, effectively elevating your mindset. By upgrading your internal operating system, you will create a mental framework that supports peak performance, not only on the golf course but in all aspects of your life.

Mindsetcaddie Reset

> **Awareness of Auto Thoughts:** Recognize and understand the role of automatic thought patterns—Auto Thoughts—in shaping your mental and emotional responses on the golf course. Identifying both constructive and destructive Auto Thoughts is crucial for improving performance.

> **Emotional Intelligence in Golf:** Developing emotional intelligence allows you to manage your emotions, stay composed under pressure, and respond thoughtfully to challenges, transforming negative situations into opportunities for growth.

> **Reprogramming Your Internal Operating System:** This book and process will guide you in updating your internal operating system by replacing outdated, limiting beliefs with empowering thoughts that enhance both mental and physical performance.

Mindsetcaddie Redirect

> As you progress through this book, you'll encounter questions and action steps designed to prompt reflection and growth. I encourage you to actively engage by using the Notes Pages provided at the back of the book,

creating a working document on your desktop, or using a journal.

> Take 10 minutes after this chapter to reflect on any internal conversations that may be preventing you from staying fully present during previous rounds of golf. What thoughts tend to surface during these moments? What expectations or outcomes are you attaching to your performance? Identify any specific thoughts that might be limiting your focus or holding you back. Once you've listed these thoughts, consider how aware you are of them—are they recurring patterns? How often do they affect your mindset on the course? What type of constructive AutoThoughts should be at the fore-front of your mind? Use this reflection as a step toward becoming more conscious of your inner dialogue and its impact on your game.

> Let's continue our habit of taking time to breathe and clear your thoughts. Find a quiet, comfortable space and sit without distractions. Close your eyes, take a deep breath, and slowly exhale, letting go of any ten-sion. Focus on your breath—notice the natural rhythm of each inhale and exhale. Allow your breathing to flow effortlessly, embracing the calm it brings. As you set-tle into this calm, you'll notice a heightened sense of emotional intelligence, becoming more aware of how you feel in the moment. This calm not only nurtures stillness but also sharpens your ability to recognize and respond to your emotions with greater clarity. As

thoughts come and go, observe them without judgment and gently return your focus to your breath. Stay present, enjoy the stillness, and let yourself simply be in the moment, attuned to both your inner peace and emotional awareness.

> As an additional reinforcement tool, you can now listen to Day Three in the audio program available on my app. I will guide you through the breathing and meditation exercise to promote calmness, awareness, and guided thought.

RELAXATION IN GOLF

We are not immune to worry, anxiety, or stress—but what truly matters is how we manage and cope when it happens.

GOLF IS A UNIQUE GAME that challenges both the body and the mind, often pushing players to their limits. It's not uncommon for a single frustrating shot or poor performance to spiral into a negative mindset that takes over the entire round. This mental struggle can overshadow the physical aspects of the game, making it harder to focus, recover, and perform at your best.

For some, the frustration becomes so overwhelming that it leads them to give up, leaving the course feeling defeated. They manifest a sense of embarrassment, allowing self-doubt and frustration to cloud their judgment, making it difficult to recover mentally or enjoy the experience.

It's common for golfers to defend a bad shot or poor performance, thinking that justifying it will somehow ease their frustration or make the outcome seem more acceptable. But how often do you hear a great golfer defend a bad shot? Hardly ever. That's because, in their minds, they're not fixated on what just happened—they're already focused on the next opportunity ahead. Pro golfers understand that each shot is just a part of the journey and dwelling on the past only detracts from future performance.

Put things in proper perspective—there is no perfect shot. Every shot, no matter where the ball lands, is an opportunity to recalibrate, refocus, and keep moving forward. A bad shot isn't the end—it's simply part of the game. Wherever the ball ends up, that's your new starting point, your next opportunity—so don't waste energy looking back.

Dwelling on mistakes does nothing but fuel frustration, distancing you from the level of play you aspire to reach. Instead, learn to embrace the imperfections and focus on what you can control: your mindset, your next move, and the progress ahead.

Don't get me wrong—all sports require mental conditioning. But golf is one of those rare sports where your mental game directly affects your physical *flow.* The connection between mind and body is so intertwined that if your thoughts aren't in the right place, your swing, stance, and even your energy on the course can suffer. That's why developing mental resilience is critical for success in golf.

To truly understand and tap into training your brain, it starts with learning to embrace relaxation, calmness, and being present. These qualities allow you to detach from past mistakes and future anxieties, keeping your focus on the moment. When your mind is centered and clear, your body naturally follows, enabling you to play with more precision, confidence, and control.

It's important to recognize how the mind works. Your mind-set—the subconscious—has been shaped and programmed by your life experiences, starting from the day you were born. This part of your brain holds the key to your habits, emotions, and reactions. It remembers your past, knows your fears, and protects you by recalling moments of failure, disappointment, or fear. This built-in protective mechanism serves as a double-edged sword on the golf course.

When you step up to take a swing, your subconscious taps into past experiences. If you've ever missed a crucial shot or doubted your ability, those memories can bubble up to the surface, subtly influencing your thoughts and actions. This is when self-doubt, tension, and fear creep in, even when you're physically prepared. That internal voice may tell you that history will repeat itself, leading to a similar result.

The good news is this: the programming of your mental "app" is not permanent. You have the power to change it, starting right now. Your thoughts, beliefs, and habits can be reprogrammed to support your goals and elevate your performance, both on and off the course. The catch? You must first learn to relax at a level deeper than you ever have before. True transformation begins when you reach a state of deep relaxation, where your mind is open and receptive to new ideas and positive change.

When you are more relaxed, you can bypass the resistance and noise of everyday thoughts, accessing the subconscious mind where real change happens. This is where the magic takes place—where you can rewire your thinking, break through mental barriers, and unlock a higher potential. It's not about forcing yourself to change; it's about allowing your mind to reset and refocus, creating new, empowering mental habits that will serve you in every area of life.

True transformation is when your mind is open and receptive to new ideas and positive change.

Relaxation will allow you to not only feel more at ease but also have the tools to take control of your mindset, reprogram negative thoughts, and replace them with empowering beliefs. This is the foundation for lasting transformation—starting with relaxation and leading to greater control, confidence, and success. In the previous few chapters, I have asked you to start a process of simply taking time to close your eyes and focus on your breathing and presence. Let's now explore the essence of directed relaxation.

The Importance of Deep Relaxation

The kind of relaxation that I am referring to goes beyond rest or leisure. This isn't about taking a break or watching a movie; it's about consciously engaging with the mind and body to create space for new possibilities. Relaxation, in this sense, is not passive—it's active, intentional, and transformative.

Relaxation allows you to override your subconscious programming by creating a clean slate—a mental reset. By letting go of preprogrammed beliefs, melting away stress, and quieting the internal chatter, you can access the powerful creative potential of your mind. Most people think they know how to relax, but very few do it in a way that engages both the body and the mind fully. Mastering this art can open doors to not only better golf but also increased personal accountability, self-discovery, and growth.

In golf, as in life, the first step toward success is eliminating doubt and fear. Relaxation is the gateway to overcoming these mental barriers, putting you in the driver's seat of your own mind. Once you understand how to relax deeply, you can begin to reprogram your thoughts and actions, ensuring that you're setting yourself up for success, not self-sabotage.

Intentional Breathing

One of the most powerful tools for relaxation is something you do every day without even thinking about it: intentional breathing. In fact, the way you breathe can be a direct reflection of your mental state. Shallow, rapid breathing often indicates stress or anxiety, while slow, deep breaths promote calm and relaxation.

This simple but vital action serves as a bridge between your mind and body, directly influencing how you feel and perform.

When you take conscious control of your breath, you send a signal to your mind and body that it's time to relax. This is especially crucial on the golf course, where maintaining a calm, clear mind can be the difference between success and failure. A cluttered mind leads to tight muscles and erratic shots, while a relaxed mind allows for fluid, focused play.

The next time you're preparing for a shot, take a moment to focus on your breathing. Inhale slowly through your nose, hold the breath for a second or two, and then exhale gently through your mouth. Repeat this process a few times, allowing each breath to quiet your mind and center your attention.

When you control your breath, you control your state of mind—a true catalyst for leveraging your mindset in golf.

During my entire career as a hypnotist, everything starts with the simple act of breathing. It is literally how we flip the switch. Whether helping individuals overcome stress, improve their mindset, or enhance their performance, controlled breathing has always been the foundation. When you control your breath, you control your state of mind, and this principle is a true catalyst in leveraging your mindset in golf.

By doing this, you activate your body's natural relaxation response. Not only does it lower your heart rate, it also reduces tension in your muscles, allowing for smoother swings and more controlled shots. Your focus sharpens, and the mental clutter that can interfere with your game begins to clear. This simple breathing technique helps you stay in the present moment—where all great golf is played.

Breathing is not just a tool for calming your nerves; it's a way to regain control when the pressure mounts. Whether you're standing on the tee box of a challenging hole or about to make a crucial putt, intentional, deep breaths remind your body to relax and your mind to stay focused. Each breath anchors you to the present, helping you let go of past mistakes or future anxieties, allowing you to approach each shot with clarity and confidence. Over time, this practice becomes second nature, giving you a powerful, reliable method to manage stress and enhance your performance on the course.

Calmness Under Pressure: Rewriting Your Mental App

Calmness is the ultimate goal in moments of high pressure. On the course, there will always be pressure—whether it's a key tournament, a challenging shot, or simply the weight of your own expectations. The AutoThoughts process is built on your ability to clear out negative or destructive thoughts and replace them with constructive ones that align with your goals and performance.

Achieving this mental shift starts with relaxation. As you breathe deeply and allow calmness to settle in, you create a space to reshape your mental narrative. Instead of fixating on past failures or worrying about potential mistakes, your mind becomes open to new, positive possibilities. Your internal dialogue shifts from, *What if I miss this shot?* to *I'm focused, calm, and capable.* This shift in thinking is crucial for resetting your mental app and taking control of your mindset, allowing you to perform at your best.

As calmness takes over, it allows you the space needed to separate from the emotional weight of the moment and make clearer, more intentional decisions. You stop reacting and start responding thoughtfully, with a mindset that supports success rather than fear of failure. This space gives you the freedom to approach each shot with confidence, knowing that the outcome doesn't define you, but your ability to remain composed does.

Calmness, however, is not just about relaxation—it's about rewriting the default responses in your mind. In high-pressure moments, your body's natural instinct may be to tighten up or react with fear, doubt, or hesitation. But through the AutoThoughts process, you can train your brain to respond with clarity and focus, rather than stress. Each breath you take serves as a reset button, allowing you to override the destructive patterns that surface under pressure.

In golf, the ability to remain calm and focused is as important as mastering your swing, if not more so. The best players don't just rely on their physical skills, they harness the power of their minds to maintain composure and clear thinking, even in the most stressful situations. This mental strength doesn't come naturally—it's cultivated through practices like controlled breathing and focused relaxation, which allow you to stay centered in the moment.

Choose to Be Calm

Taking charge of your breath is the first step in reclaiming your focus. Each deep, intentional breath grounds you in the present, calming your nervous system and quieting the mental noise that can sabotage your game. When you breathe with purpose, you also shift your perspective—recognizing that every shot is an opportunity, not a challenge to fear. In this state of calm, you become more adaptable, able to handle whatever lies ahead without being thrown off course by nerves or frustration.

The ability to remain calm under pressure is the ultimate advantage. It keeps you grounded, focused, and in control, no matter how high the stakes. By mastering your breath, resetting your mental app, and reframing your thoughts, you set yourself up for success not only on the golf course but in life as well.

I remember the first football team I ever hypnotized was the University of Southern California (USC) team. It was a Saturday in August when former head coach Pete Carroll called me, asking me to come do my show and talk about the power of mindset. I asked, "When are you thinking?" and he replied, "How about Tuesday?" The rest was history. But what I remember most wasn't just the event itself, but the experience of standing there, all 5' 7" and 165 pounds of me, surrounded by players three times my size. These massive linemen towered over me like I was an ant. But that never fazed me.

The program was incredible. These huge, tough athletes dropped like flies as I hypnotized them, and they were having a blast as I demonstrated the power of suggestion and the world of guided imagery. What stood out as the key to the entire experience was calmness. Calmness allowed them to embrace the process, trust their minds, and fully engage. It doesn't matter who you are or how big the challenge is—when you are calm, everything seems clear. Calmness gives you a playing field that is unlimited—whether you're on the golf course or in the midst of life's challenges, it's the foundation for achieving anything.

Relaxation as a Daily Practice

Achieving deep relaxation doesn't happen instantly—it takes time and consistent practice. Yet, the effects of relaxation are undeniably unlimited. When you incorporate relaxation techniques into your daily routine, it has the potential to not only sharpen your golf game but also positively influence your overall well-being. Relaxation works by lowering stress levels, boosting focus, and supporting both mental and physical recovery. As you calm your body and mind, you allow yourself to operate at a higher level of productivity and performance.

When you relax, tension melts away, and this allows your mind to focus more clearly. It helps reduce the noise of daily stressors, leaving space for better decision-making and concentration. Your heart rate slows, and your body produces fewer stress hormones, both of which are essential to performing optimally, whether you're on the course or in everyday life. That's why so many successful people make relaxation part of their daily habits—they understand its role in keeping them sharp, focused, and resilient under pressure.

By setting aside a few minutes each day to relax intentionally, this time allows you to focus on deep breathing, clear away distractions, and release any tension you're holding on to. As you practice this consistently, relaxation will become second nature, and you can call on that calm whenever needed.

Mastering the ability to relax gives you an edge.

Whether you're about to take an important shot in golf or managing the challenges of daily life, mastering the ability to relax will give you an edge. Over time, this practice will transform how you respond to stress, allowing you to remain composed, centered, and fully present no matter the situation. Relaxation is not just a wish or hope, it should be a necessity for overall mindfulness.

As you become more proficient in leveraging your mindset, you will implement your breath, calmness, and relaxation into your journey. By focusing on your breath and allowing yourself to relax fully, you are taking the first step in rewriting your mental app. This clean slate will give you the power to approach each round of golf with calmness, confidence, and control.

Remember, relaxation is not just a one-time fix—it's a lifestyle, a daily habit that can transform the way you think, feel, and perform on the course. Commit to practicing deep relaxation, and watch as your mindset, game, and life begin to change. Breathe, relax, and take command of your game. The possibilities are endless.

By investing in yourself and applying these principles, you create a balance that allows you to achieve true presence. All golfers know that being fully present in every part of the game puts you in the zone where flow happens naturally without overthinking. It's where your mind directs the ball, and your body instinctively follows.

MindsetCaddie Reset

> **Release Mental Barriers:** In golf, your breath and calmness allow you to clear mental clutter, reset your

mindset, and approach each shot with focus and confidence, free from the baggage of past mistakes.

> **Intentional Breathing:** Mastering your breath is key to maintaining mental clarity and calmness under pressure, enabling you to reprogram your thoughts and prevent self-sabotage on the course.

> **Consistent Practice:** Developing a daily practice of deep relaxation not only enhances your mental resilience in golf but also promotes overall well-being, unlocking greater control, precision, and flow in your game.

MindsetCaddie Redirect

> When you're on the course and face a stressful situation, use your breathing as a reset. Before taking your next shot, pause and take a few deep breaths, releasing any frustration or anxiety. Approach the shot with a calm and focused mindset, just as you practiced during your relaxation sessions.

> Make relaxation an essential part of your pre-shot routine and daily life. Over time, this practice will help you stay calm under pressure, allowing you to perform with greater confidence, clarity, and control on the golf course and in life. By incorporating this simple yet

powerful practice, you can control your mindset and reset your mental app whenever you need it, unlocking your full potential.

> Let's maintain our practice of taking time to breathe and clear your mind. Find a quiet, comfortable spot where you can sit undisturbed. Close your eyes, take a deep breath in, and exhale slowly, releasing any tension. Focus on your breath, noticing the natural rhythm as you inhale and exhale. Let your breathing flow smoothly, welcoming the sense of calm it brings. If any thoughts arise, simply observe them without judgment, and gently bring your attention back to your breath. Stay grounded in the moment, enjoy the stillness, and allow yourself to just be.

> As an additional reinforcement tool, you can now listen to Day Four in the audio program available on my app. I will guide you through the breathing and meditation exercise to promote calmness, awareness, and guided thought.

WHO IS WINNING WITH HYPNOSIS IN GOLF

Believe it is possible. To be a winner, first
you have to believe you can be one!

IT IS NO SECRET that professional golfers have long
integrated hypnosis, meditation, guided imagery, and mindset
training into their routines as part of their overall success. These
tools are not just supplemental but essential for unlocking mental resilience, focus, and consistency. In golf, where the mental
game is just as crucial as physical skills, top players have turned
to these techniques to elevate their performance and maintain
an edge.

Many legendary players have embraced the power of mental
conditioning, including hypnosis, to enhance their game. The following case studies highlight how some of the greatest golfers in
history used these techniques to shape their careers.

Tiger Woods: Mental Toughness and Hypnosis from an Early Age

From a young age, Tiger Woods recognized the importance of mental toughness. He was introduced to meditation and self-hypnosis by his father, who believed in the power of the mind to achieve greatness. Woods used these techniques to maintain intense focus during high-pressure moments, block out distractions, and develop an unshakable belief in his abilities. Throughout his career, this mental conditioning has allowed him to come back from adversity, overcome injuries, and remain one of the most dominant players in golf history. His ability to stay calm and composed under the most intense circumstances is a testament to his mental preparation.

Phil Mickelson: Strategic Thinking and Mental Preparation

Phil Mickelson's career has been defined by his ability to think strategically, adapt to changing conditions, and maintain a positive mindset even in the face of setbacks. While Mickelson's talent is undeniable, he attributes much of his success to his mental preparation. Hypnosis and visualization have been key components of his mental training, helping him stay confident, sharp, and resilient. His consistent success over decades is proof of the power of mental conditioning, which allows him to remain calm and make smart decisions, no matter the pressure.

Jack Nicklaus: Visualization and Mental Discipline

Jack Nicklaus, one of the greatest golfers of all time, has often spoken about the importance of visualization in his career. Nicklaus would mentally rehearse each shot before he took it, seeing the ball's trajectory, visualizing the swing, and imagining the perfect outcome. This mental discipline became a cornerstone of his game, helping him remain focused and confident on the course. Hypnosis-like techniques, such as this deep mental rehearsal, allowed him to maintain his poise and perform with precision, even in the most high-stakes moments. Nicklaus's legendary career is a testament to the power of the mind in shaping success.

Hypnosis in Action: Cameron Davis's Career Turnaround

One of the most compelling examples of hypnosis in action comes from the story of Cameron Davis, an Australian golfer who used these techniques to turn his career around. Davis had reached a career low, struggling with his performance and battling mental barriers that kept him from realizing his full potential. He had lost confidence in his ability to compete at the highest level and was considering giving up.

However, through dedicated mindset coaching and hypnosis, Davis was able to break free from his mental obstacles. By using hypnosis to eliminate self-doubt, reduce anxiety, and refocus his energy on success, he gradually regained his confidence. The mental shift he experienced was dramatic, allowing him to approach the game with renewed determination and clarity.

The results speak for themselves. Cameron Davis not only overcame his career slump but also went on to achieve a stunning victory on the PGA Tour. In 2024, Davis clinched the Rocket Mortgage Classic, further demonstrating the lasting power of hypnosis and mental conditioning in achieving consistent success on the golf course. His story is a powerful reminder that mastering the mental game can be the key to unlocking peak performance.

You Are Next!

Your journey through this book and coaching began the moment you started reading. You've delved into mindset techniques, learned the critical importance of relaxation, and witnessed how mental conditioning has shaped the success of some of the greatest golfers in history. But now, it's time to shift the focus to you. This is your opportunity to take the lessons you've absorbed and apply them directly to your own game.

As you move forward, you will develop a personalized mental blueprint that aligns with your strengths, aspirations, and challenges. The techniques you've learned will not only transform your performance on the course but also foster a mindset of resilience, confidence, and focus that extends into every aspect of your life. Now is the time to embrace the power of your mind and commit to unlocking your full potential, one thought, one breath, and one swing at a time.

I want to ask you a question, but more importantly, I want *you* to ask yourself this question: *What is it that I truly want?* Specifically, what do you want from your golf game?

At first glance, this might seem like a simple question. But I challenge you to think deeper. What *exactly* do you want to achieve? Is it to break a personal scoring barrier? To remain calm and composed when everything is on the line? To become a more consistent player, or to simply enjoy the game without the frustration that holds you back?

Take a moment to reflect on what success looks like to you. Does it mean dominating your local club tournaments? Beating your personal best round? Or maybe it's about stepping onto the course with absolute confidence, knowing that no matter what, you're in control.

Let's be real: *Do you want to win?* Don't shy away from that ambition! There's nothing wrong with wanting to win, with embracing that competitive fire. In fact, you *should* want to win. Saying it out loud, believing it deep down, is the first step toward making it a reality.

You're not just another golfer hoping to get better. You're reading this book because you want to elevate your game. You're reading because you know there's more potential within you waiting to be unlocked. And let me tell you, the path to unlocking that potential doesn't begin with your physical skills—it begins in your mind.

What I'm telling you is this: **winning starts with believing.** It's not about believing when you see it; it's about knowing that you'll see it when you believe it. That belief has to be unshakable. You have to wake up every day *knowing* you're capable of achieving the results you want, regardless of the setbacks you may have faced in the past.

This is where your mental app comes into play. You have the ability to rewrite it, to break free from the limiting beliefs that have held you back, and to take control of your mental game. The doubts, the fears, the frustrations—they're not permanent. They're not part of who you are, unless you allow them to be. You have the power to change the narrative.

Think about it: every great golfer you admire—Tiger, Phil, Jack—they didn't achieve greatness by accident. They did it because they mastered their mindset. They believed in their vision before anyone else did, and they backed that belief with action. They saw the course, visualized their shots, and trusted that they could execute. You have that same power within you.

You've already taken the first steps by committing to this journey. You've done the hard part by showing up, by recognizing that there's more to be discovered in your game. Now, it's time to go further.

This Is Your Opportunity to Rise

It's time to apply what you've learned—relaxation, visualization, focus—and start rewriting the story in your head. The mental game isn't some mystical concept, it's a skill; and like any skill, it can be developed. And when you master it, everything changes. Your confidence, your ability to handle pressure, your joy on the course—it all becomes elevated.

But here's the key to elevating your mental game—it requires action. You can't just read about these techniques—you need to implement them. Make mindset training part of your daily routine. Meditate, visualize your success, practice your breathing techniques before each round. The work you do off the course is just as important as what happens on it. The real transformation happens when you commit to making your mental game a priority.

Ask yourself:

> ❯ *Am I ready to take control of my game?*
> ❯ *Am I ready to believe in myself and step into the winner's mindset?*

If the answer is yes, then it's time to act. You already have the tools, the knowledge, and the desire. Now it's time to bring it all together. You're standing on the edge of something great, and the only thing left to do is step forward. Winning is not some distant goal; it's within your grasp. All you need is the belief, the commitment, and the action to make it happen.

So, ask yourself again: *What do I truly want?* And once you've answered, go after it with everything you've got. Your future in this game is unlimited, and the journey starts right now.

MindsetCaddie Reset

> **Train Like the Pros:** Professional golfers have used hypnosis, meditation, and visualization to master mental resilience and elevate their game. It is now your time to embrace these skills to enhance your performance and outcomes.

> **Train Like a Winner:** As you apply the mindset techniques you've learned, visualizing success and embracing your ambitions, you can rewrite your mental narrative, unlock your full potential, and take control of your game—and your life—one step at a time.

> **Embrace the Process:** Mental conditioning is not just a supplement but a core part of a golfer's success, helping them stay calm, focused, and confident under pressure. Remember that each chapter/day is part of the process. Stay committed and trust in your growth, knowing that every step forward brings you closer to new opportunities and the success you envision.

Mindsetcaddie Redirect

> Grab a piece of paper and a pen. Write a bold permission statement that reflects your intention. For example, write, "I give myself permission to win!" Sign it. This act is your key to turning your intention into reality. The mind works based on what it is thinking about, and by putting your intention in writing, you're giving your mind a clear and powerful focus. This physical act reinforces your mental commitment, aligning your thoughts with your desired outcome. Keep this statement where you can see it daily, as a reminder that you've given yourself permission to step into your best self and manifest your goals. Your mind will continually shape your actions based on what it is focused on, so let this serve as the anchor for your thoughts, guiding you toward success.

> Take 10 minutes to practice intentional deep relaxation. Sit quietly, focus on your breathing—inhale deeply through your nose, hold briefly, and exhale slowly. Use this time to clear your mind of any distractions or past mistakes, setting yourself up to be fully present for your next round of golf. Yes, take the time and train your brain to be more relaxed, calm, and present. During this personal time. Think about your "I am" statement. Reflect on it. Embrace it. Engrave it into your mindset.

❭ As a reinforcement tool, you can now listen to Day Five in the audio program in my app. I will guide you through the breathing and meditation exercise to promote calmness, awareness, and guided thought, adding elements based on this chapter.

THE MECHANICS AND MINDSET (M & M) OF GOLF

Today, replace one limiting belief
with an empowering affirmation
by making a deliberate shift.

YOU LOVE GOLF but don't love carrying the bag of frustration, lack of confidence, and negative self-talk. Golf is a game many people love, yet they often don't enjoy playing it as much as they could. Why? Frustration, lack of confidence, self-doubt, and negative self-talk can cloud what should be a pleasurable experience. But here's the truth: you can overcome these mental barriers and rediscover your love for the game by addressing both the mechanics and mindset (M & M) of golf.

To overcome these challenges, it's essential to engage both your physical and mental game:

> **Mechanics**—your swing, grip, stance, and technique—are vital, but they only take you so far.

> **Mindset**—your mental resilience and confidence—is equally important.

Together, M & M are your partners on the course. You can't reach your full potential by focusing on one and neglecting the other. This is why the game of golf is won by two essential partners: Mechanics and Mindset.

This chapter expands on the concept of leveraging your mindset, much like the way you focus on mastering the physical mechanics of the game. I break this down into short updates, each highlighting a specific aspect of mindset. As you go through each one, take a moment to reflect on what resonates with you personally—what stands out to you will be the most relevant to your own game and growth.

Here's one important reminder: *integrating mindset as a key partner to mechanics should feel natural, not overwhelming.* This approach isn't meant to be just another item on your to-do list or something you need to constantly manage. Instead, it's an essential element that complements your physical skills, enhancing your performance without dominating your focus.

Think of mindset as the foundation that supports everything you've already built in your game. By gradually weaving mental resilience, clarity, and confidence into your practice, you will start to feel their benefits instinctively. It's about allowing mindset to become a steady, guiding force—one that strengthens your mechanics, adds to your enjoyment of the game, and elevates your growth without ever feeling like an additional task.

"Your mindset is a steady, guiding force that strengthens your mechanics, adds to your enjoyment, and elevates your growth.

As we have already discussed, golfers battle an invisible adversary—a mental wall constructed from negative self-talk, frustration, and doubt. It's easy to get caught in this cycle, but it's also preventable. We can train our minds just as we train our bodies, breaking through these barriers and transforming how we approach the game. Remember, it's not just about perfecting your swing; it's about aligning your mind and body to perform in harmony.

Here's how to engage both your mechanics and mindset for maximum success on the course. The key lies in recognizing that every physical action on the course is influenced by your mental state. When frustration or doubt creeps in, it impacts your mechanics, throwing off timing, precision, and fluidity. Conversely, when you focus on positive self-talk, relaxation, and staying in the moment, you create an environment where both your mind and body can operate at their highest potential.

By integrating mental conditioning with physical practice, your swing becomes more natural and instinctive, and you will recover from mistakes faster. It's about creating consistency—not just in your technique, but in your thought patterns. Through visualization, controlled breathing, and staying present, you can train your mind to work in sync with your body, unlocking a flow state where confidence replaces fear, and doubt gives way to trust. This alignment is what truly elevates your performance, helping you achieve your peak game, round after round.

As you work with both mechanics and mindset, think of them as elements you're adding to a software program. You might not need every line of code, but each part strengthens the program, making it more versatile and resilient—like building a robust security firewall. Similarly, integrating mechanics and mindset doesn't have to feel overwhelming; it simply fortifies your game, creating a balanced, high-performing system.

Daily Software Updates

Acknowledge and Isolate Limiting Beliefs

Before your next round, take a moment to identify any negative thoughts or doubts. Acknowledge them, but don't dwell on them. Mentally place them in a corner, separate from your focus.

This exercise will help you compartmentalize and prevent these thoughts from affecting your performance.

Positive Affirmations

Replace negative self-talk with positive affirmations. Reinforce your confidence with statements like "I trust my swing," "I am calm under pressure," and "I've got this." These affirmations will rewire your mindset to support your game, rather than undermine it.

Visualization

Spend time visualizing your success on the course. See yourself making perfect shots and handling challenging situations with confidence. This mental rehearsal sets a positive tone for your game and strengthens your belief in your abilities.

Be Present

Stay focused on the present shot. If you find yourself distracted by frustration or self-doubt, acknowledge it, set it aside, and refocus on the moment. Breathing techniques can help you regain calm and keep your mind clear.

Developing Resilience

Like any habit, resilience is built through repetition. The more you practice these mental techniques, the more automatic they become, just like your swing. Your goal is to develop a seamless connection between your mechanics and mindset—a mental operating system that supports your performance without conscious effort.

Pre-Round Routine: Incorporate mental preparation into your pre-round routine. Spend a few minutes meditating, visualizing your best shots, and using positive affirmations to reinforce your confidence.

During the Round: Stay mindful and focused. If limiting beliefs arise, acknowledge them, set them aside, and refocus on the task at hand. Deep breathing will help you remain calm and centered.

Post-Round Reflection: Reflect on your performance. Identify moments when limiting beliefs affected your game, and consider how you can address them next time. This reflection will help you continuously improve both your mechanics and mindset.

Each of the suggested "software updates" I've recommended isn't required but serves as a reference for what might resonate with you. The more you're exposed to these concepts, the more they can become ingrained, gradually shaping your approach.

Think of it like traveling and adapting to new cities, as you've done throughout your life. Over time, living in different places becomes second nature; you find yourself feeling at home, almost as if you'd been there for years. Similarly, as you immerse yourself in these mindset practices, they become familiar, seamlessly blending into your approach and making it feel like a natural part of your game and growth.

The Power of Your Inner Voice

The key to keeping your mechanics and mindset in sync is your inner voice. It works together with your "Mind's Eye"—your mental imagery system that ties stored visuals with other sensory inputs—to shape your reality. Think of it as your inner caddie. For example, imagine you're frustrated after a missed putt.

Instead of letting the frustration grow, find a quiet moment, close your eyes, and use your inner voice to shift the narrative. Visualize a perfect putt rolling smoothly into the hole. By focusing on this positive mental image, you guide your mindset toward confidence and calm. That's the power of your inner voice, and it's what many golfers—just like top athletes in other fields—use to boost their performance, even if they don't call it by that name.

Your inner voice can turn your visualized outcomes into reality.

Visualization is essential in creating a winning mindset in golf. Your inner voice paints mental pictures that work just like actual visual inputs—the brain doesn't know the difference between what's real and what's imagined. When your Mind's Eye "sees" something, like sinking that tricky putt, it starts to feel achievable. Your internal dialogue shifts, and suddenly that scenario becomes more real. With each repetition, your inner voice strengthens the belief that you can succeed, helping to turn your visualized outcomes into reality.

How Does This Work?

The human brain, while complex, responds to visualizations. Research shows that the brain treats imagined scenarios like real memories. This means that when you mentally rehearse a perfect swing or a clutch putt, your brain interprets it as if you've actually done it. Later, when you're on the course, your brain recalls this "experience," and you approach the situation with more confidence and clarity. Your brain believes that these visual images are possible, because to it, they're already memories.

Let's say you're struggling with tee shots. Picture yourself stepping up to the tee, feeling calm and in control. Visualize a smooth, powerful swing, and watch the ball soar straight down the fairway. Your brain stores this imagined experience as a memory. So when you actually tee up, you feel less pressure and more confidence, as if you've done it successfully countless times before.

In my coaching sessions, I often guide golfers through this process. I ask them to focus on an image or sensation that makes them feel relaxed—like the feel of the club in their hands or the sound of the ball dropping into the cup. Once they've built that calming picture, I have them apply those same sensations to a situation on the course that typically causes frustration or nerves. By combining these positive emotions with the challenging situation, they rewire their mindset to approach the game with more ease and focus. This is the synergy between the inner voice and the mind's eye—using mental imagery and positive self-talk to guide yourself toward the outcome you want.

Your Inner Voice Updates

The concept behind using your inner voice is rooted in the connection between your mind and body. Just as your body reacts to physical sensations like sights and sounds, your mind responds to the things you visualize, even if they aren't real yet. This technique has been used by golfers to mentally rehearse their game, ease performance anxiety, and enhance focus before critical shots. By vividly imagining success, you change the way you approach the game—and that shift in mindset translates into better performance.

For example, if you visualize yourself executing the perfect shot, sinking a long putt, or hitting that approach shot exactly where you want it to land, your brain starts to believe these outcomes are possible. With each mental "rehearsal," your body follows suit, improving your game. Your Inner Voice works by reinforcing these positive mental images, which help to build confidence, consistency, and resilience.

Your inner voice puts you in control of your golf game. You can consciously choose the mental images and suggestions that will propel you toward success. Whether you want to improve your swing, your putting, or simply your attitude on the course, your inner voice is there to help. The path you take is entirely up to you.

By tapping into your inner voice, you can improve your golf performance, attitude, and overall well-being. When you use it to relax before a round, your inner voice can lower your stress levels, ease nerves, and sharpen your focus. It's like a mental dress rehearsal that gets you ready for the actual game. You can use it to prepare for every hole, every swing, and every putt, visualizing yourself executing each with precision. It's your voice—use it to drive your success on the course.

Visualization

There are many strategies you can use to integrate visualization into your golf routine. One is to create a "vision board" displaying images that inspire you—maybe photos of great golfers or beautiful courses. Looking at these images regularly keeps your goals at the forefront of your mind, reinforcing them in your subconscious. Over time, your mindset aligns with these images, helping you reach your goals with greater ease and confidence.

By imagining yourself nailing that perfect drive or sinking a long putt, these outcomes become more attainable. Your brain helps keep that goal alive and prominent during your round, leading to better focus and consistency. The more you see what you want, the more your subconscious mind works to bring it into reality.

Using your inner voice is about giving your mind the right suggestions, so your body and emotions respond as if you are already experiencing your desired outcomes. If your mind can see it, your body can achieve it. Once your inner voice aligns your mind's eye with your goals, the possibilities for your golf game are limitless!

"Mastering the mechanics and your mindset eliminates frustration, boosts confidence, and enhances your overall golfing experience.

By mastering both the mechanics and mindset of golf, you can eliminate frustration, boost your confidence, and enhance your overall experience on the course. The wall you once faced becomes a stepping stone to greater success. Remember, your mind is your most powerful tool, and when mechanics and mindset work together, there's no limit to what you can achieve.

Mindsetcaddie Reset

> **Deliberate Shift:** Mastering both the physical mechanics and mental aspects of golf is crucial for overcoming challenges like frustration, lack of confidence, and self-doubt, enabling you to reach your full potential and enjoy the game more.

> **Weaving Mental Resilience:** Incorporating mental techniques such as visualization, positive affirmations, and mindfulness during each shot can help you reframe negative self-talk and improve focus, leading to a more consistent and confident performance.

> **Your Inner Voice:** When aligned with mental imagery and positive reinforcement, your inner voice becomes a powerful tool for transforming visualized successes into reality. It fosters resilience and helps you stay calm under pressure on the course.

Mindsetcaddie Redirect

> Are you setting aside time each day to connect with your inner voice? Spend a few minutes writing a brief description of your ideal golf moments. By visualizing yourself hitting that perfect drive or sinking a long putt, you make those outcomes feel more achievable. Your brain keeps these goals at the forefront of your mind throughout your round, enhancing your focus and consistency. The more you envision what you want, the more your subconscious mind works to turn it into reality.

> Take a moment now to close your eyes and visualize what you just wrote down. This is a mental exercise— simple, yet powerful. Don't underestimate its impact.

> As a reinforcement tool, you can now listen to Day Six in the audio program in my app. I will guide you through the breathing and meditation exercise to promote calmness, awareness, and guided thought, adding elements based on this chapter.

THE POWER OF PAUSE

The danger of assumptions in golf is that they create a false sense of certainty about your performance. Challenge your assumptions regularly to avoid complacency and foster a mindset of curiosity and open-mindedness.

HOW OFTEN HAVE YOU seen a golfer express disappointment with an ugh, a grunt, or a grimace? Or has this happened to you? Your reaction can either hold you back or propel you forward. When you're playing golf with others, how attuned are you to their reactions when they drive, chip, or putt? How do they respond? Understanding and being aware of these reactions is crucial for your own performance.

But what does your reaction really do? It has the power to influence your mindset, your focus, and even the energy you bring to the game. Is it really helpful or harmful to react? Your reaction can either reinforce positive momentum or create unnecessary obstacles. By recognizing and managing your reactions, you not only enhance your own performance, you also set the tone for how you handle challenges and successes on the course. This awareness becomes a vital tool in maintaining composure, building confidence, and keeping your game moving in the right direction.

If your actions on the course result in something you're displeased with, it's essential to resist the urge to react impulsively. Reacting with frustration or disappointment can spiral into negative self-talk and distract you from the task at hand. When your mind is caught up in disappointment, you're not truly present. Your mind acts on the last message you send it, and frustration can dominate your thoughts as you try to either defend your actions or anticipate a negative outcome that hasn't even happened yet. Instead, *take a moment to pause and refocus.*

Yes, PAUSE. Accept the outcome, and move forward with a clear mind. The key is to maintain emotional control and not let one moment define your entire game. By choosing not to react negatively, you preserve your mental energy, stay in the present, and give yourself the best chance to recover and perform at your highest level.

Change is a constant in playing golf. The need to adapt and evolve is ever-present, from weather to the greens. However, the most profound and impactful shifts often stem from within—specifically, from the mindset of the player. Leveraging your mindset to enhance your game isn't about how far you drive the ball; it's about a transformational journey of being present and in complete control of your mindset. It's the lens through which you view challenges, setbacks, and opportunities.

This means recognizing that *every experience, whether positive or negative, is an opportunity to learn and evolve.* It's about understanding that you are not fixed in your ways but are in a state of constant growth. This mindset is not just about being open to change—it's about actively seeking it out, embracing it, and using it as a catalyst for being in complete harmony when playing.

Nothing significant happens overnight. Every advanced golfer knows that success is a culmination of days, months, and often years of hard work, dedication, and perseverance. But more than just time and effort, success is about the mindset with which you approach each day. It's about understanding that every day is a process, a step in the journey toward achieving your goals.

Overcoming mental barriers is not just about making minor tweaks or adjustments to your strategies. It's about a profound and fundamental shift in perceiving, thinking, and operating. It's about letting go of limiting beliefs and *embracing a mindset that sees challenges as opportunities, failures as lessons, and change as a chance to grow and thrive.*

The mental wall that sometimes builds up needs to be broken down to develop a higher ability to unlock the potential within, break free from self-imposed barriers, and chart a course toward becoming a calm, resilient, and talented golfer.

If we continuously react in the same way, we remain rooted in repeating that action. Often, we don't even realize the habits that are fueling our mental barriers. It's only when we truly observe our patterns and habits that we can acknowledge the need for change.

Create a Pattern Interrupter

This is where the PAUSE becomes truly powerful. A Pattern Interrupter is a conscious action or thought that breaks the cycle of automatic behavior, allowing you to step out of your habitual responses. These automatic behaviors are often driven by our AutoThoughts—those immediate, unconscious reactions that guide your actions without you even realizing it. When you feel the urge to react, take a deep breath.

This simple act of breathing serves as your Pattern Interrupter, disrupting the cycle of AutoThoughts and giving you a moment to reset. As you breathe, focus on the present moment, allowing yourself to break free from the habitual responses that may be holding you back. The PAUSE, combined with a deep breath, gives you the space to choose a more constructive response, empowering you to shift your mindset and approach challenges with greater clarity and control.

All too often, we're told to "relax" when faced with challenges or stress. While this is sound advice, it's more of a command than a technique. Simply telling yourself to relax doesn't necessarily provide the means to actually do so. This is when the PAUSE and the act of taking a breath come into play.

Instead of just telling yourself to relax, take a moment to PAUSE, inhale deeply, and then exhale slowly. This deliberate action of breathing not only serves as your Pattern Interrupter but also as a technique to genuinely relax your mind and body. The breath is your tool to create calm amidst pressure, allowing you to reset your thoughts and emotions. By focusing on your breath, you activate your body's natural relaxation response, making it easier to let go of tension and approach the situation with a clear, composed mindset.

PAUSE: Take a deep breath and exhale. Be conscious of how the air flows in and out. Be aware of the effect it has on your present moment.

Implementing this approach will not only have a profound impact on your golf game, it will also create positive ripple effects in your personal and professional life. By mastering the art of pausing, breathing, and breaking free from automatic reactions on the course, you're cultivating a powerful skill set that transcends golf.

In your personal life, these techniques can help you navigate challenging situations with greater patience and clarity, whether it's dealing with a stressful family situation or managing emotions during a difficult conversation. The ability to pause and breathe before reacting allows you to respond thoughtfully rather than impulsively, leading to healthier relationships and better decision-making.

A "PAUSE" routine helps you manage stress, communicate clearly, and lead with greater confidence and emotional intelligence.

In your professional life, this practice can be equally transformative. In high-pressure environments where quick decisions are often required, the ability to maintain composure and clarity of thought is invaluable. By incorporating a PAUSE into your routine, you can manage stress more effectively, communicate more clearly, and lead with greater confidence and emotional intelligence.

Ultimately, the skills you develop on the golf course—pausing, breathing, and breaking free from AutoThoughts—become life skills that enhance your overall well-being, effectiveness, and success in every area of your life. This holistic approach to mindset not only improves your game but also helps you become a more resilient, focused, and balanced individual both on and off the course.

A PAUSE is so powerful and effective that it naturally promotes self-reflection. When you take a moment to pause and breathe, you create space not only to calm your mind but also to gain deeper insights into your thoughts and emotions. This reflective pause allows you to step back from the immediate situation and observe your reactions more objectively.

In these moments of stillness, you can better understand the underlying triggers of your automatic responses and assess whether they are serving you or holding you back. This self-reflection fosters greater self-awareness, helping you to recognize patterns in your behavior and make more conscious choices moving forward. Over time, this practice can lead to significant personal growth and a more mindful approach to both your game and your life.

Self-reflection also opens the door to guided imagery, a powerful mental technique where you visualize desired outcomes or scenarios in vivid detail. By reflecting on your experiences and responses, you can use guided imagery to mentally rehearse positive behaviors and successful outcomes. This practice not only reinforces the mindset shifts you're working toward but also helps you build confidence and clarity in your goals. Guided imagery, rooted in the self-awareness gained through reflection, becomes a tool to actively shape your mental landscape, preparing you to face challenges with a calm and focused mind.

It's important to remember that everyone experiences setbacks—both on the golf course and in life. The goal isn't to avoid these challenges but to learn from them. Each setback is an opportunity to grow, to refine your approach, and to strengthen your mental resilience. Through the practice of pausing, breathing, and engaging in self-reflection, you cultivate the ability to view setbacks not as failures, but as valuable lessons that guide you toward improvement.

Progress is not about perfection but about consistent effort. It's the small, steady steps you take every day that lead to significant growth over time. By integrating self-compassion into your mindset, you allow yourself the grace to make mistakes, learn from them, and keep moving forward. Self-compassion means acknowledging that setbacks are a natural part of life's journey and that treating yourself with kindness and understanding during these times is crucial for long-term joy and success.

When you combine the power of PAUSE, self-reflection, guided imagery, and self-compassion, you create a resilient foundation that supports continuous progress. This approach not only helps you recover from setbacks but also propels you forward with a stronger, more confident mindset. Whether on the golf course or in any other area of life, this combination of practices equips you to navigate challenges with grace and emerge from them more empowered than before. This again reinforces your mindset caddie to act on your positive intentions, direction, and reality.

When you are more in control of your internal program, adapting to change is no longer a challenge but rather an opportunity. In golf, just as in life, unexpected outcomes are inevitable, but your mindset shapes how you respond. How often have you said, "Where the ball lands is now my opportunity"? Let me be crystal clear: no matter how skilled you are as a golfer, it is critical to accept where the ball lands and move forward by being fully present.

This perspective shift allows you to embrace whatever comes your way, seeing it not as an obstacle but as a chance to adjust, improve, and grow. When you view every outcome as an opportunity, you're no longer thrown off course by the unexpected—you remain grounded, focused, and ready to capitalize on the next move. This mindset turns every moment, even those that seem unfavorable, into a stepping stone toward success.

Mindsetcaddie Reset

> **Awareness:** Your reaction has the power to either propel you forward or create unnecessary obstacles, making awareness and control of your responses crucial for maintaining composure and confidence.

> **PAUSE to Breathe, and Reflect**: When you PAUSE you can break free from automatic reactions, allowing you to approach challenges with a clear and focused mindset, both on the golf course and in life.

> **New Perspective:** Viewing every outcome as an opportunity rather than an obstacle transforms setbacks into stepping stones for growth, helping you stay grounded, adaptable, and ready for success.

Mindsetcaddie Redirect

> Implement the "PAUSE and breathe" technique to break negative cycles. When you feel frustration or disappointment on the course, take a moment to PAUSE, take a deep breath, and then slowly exhale. This Pattern Interrupter will help you break free from automatic reactions driven by negative AutoThoughts. Focus on the present moment and reset your mindset

before taking your next shot. This practice will not only enhance your game but will help you approach challenges with greater clarity and emotional control.

> Challenge assumptions and cultivate curiosity for growth. Regularly question your assumptions about your golf performance to avoid complacency. Embrace a mindset of curiosity and openness, viewing every outcome as an opportunity to learn and improve. This approach will help you break through mental barriers, allowing you to remain adaptable and focused on continuous growth, both on and off the course.

> As a reinforcement tool, you can now listen to Day Seven in the audio program in my app. I will guide you through the breathing and meditation exercise to promote calmness, awareness, and guided thought, adding elements based on this chapter.

ANCHORING A PEAK PERFORMANCE STATE OF MIND

The words we use have the power to transform us in so many different directions. Be conscious of your internal voice!

HAVE YOU EVER HAD an incredible round of golf where everything just clicked? You were completely in the zone, fully present, and on fire. But then, a few days or a week later, you play again, and suddenly you're off your game. It happens. You still have the skills and talent, but one bad drive seems to derail the rest of your round.

Now, think about watching a tournament where a pro hits a shot that's completely out of character—a shank, perhaps—but the pro calmly approaches the ball and plays it as if completely under control. Pros aren't frustrated or emotional; they're just in the zone, fully immersed in the moment. That's what I'm talking about when I refer to being in the "now" or in a "state of flow." The ability to stay present and composed, regardless of the situation, is what allows these players to turn a potential setback into just another part of the game.

The principles of this book focus on relaxation, mental clarity, and instilling a clear sense of direction. By embracing mindfulness and staying fully engaged in the present moment, you can significantly enhance your performance. Just as training muscle memory leads to automatic physical responses, training your mind allows it to operate on autopilot, effortlessly guiding your reactions, attitude, calmness, and confidence. This mental conditioning enables you to stay present, free from the influence of negative internal or external thoughts, allowing you to perform at your best without distraction.

I'm sure you're asking yourself one or all of the following questions:

> How do I make sure I'm in the zone?

> How do I get back into it when challenges arise?

> How do I turn challenges into opportunities?

I'm here to tell you that it's easier than you think once you show yourself an alternative to what you might have been doing in the past. Meaning, nothing will change if you continue to repeat the same patterns, habits, or thoughts. You do have the remote to your emotional control.

A consistent pre-shot routine is vital for success in golf. It creates a mental and physical rhythm that prepares you for each shot, allowing you to focus fully on execution. As you update your Mindset Caddie's internal operating system software with positive AutoThoughts, you can develop and maintain a pre-shot routine that becomes second nature, even under pressure—yes, without thinking about it.

Imagine yourself performing it flawlessly, from addressing the ball to executing the shot. As you visualize, use hypnotic suggestions to embed this routine deeply into your subconscious. The goal is to make your pre-shot routine so ingrained that it becomes automatic, allowing you to rely on it even in high-pressure situations.

Staying in the present moment is key to performing well in golf. To play amazingly all the time, you must be fully present, not distracted by past mistakes or future outcomes—entirely focused on the shot in front of you. From the beginning of this book, examples and exercises have been provided to help you achieve this level of focus consistently.

I'm not suggesting that you change your pre-shot routine or add another thing to worry about. Instead, I encourage you to become in tune with your pre-shot routine, trusting your talent and staying present. Mindfulness in golf means being aware of your thoughts, feelings, and surroundings without getting caught up in them. It's about maintaining a calm, focused mind that stays in the moment. Leveraging your mindset daily can deepen this mindfulness, helping you tune into the present moment more fully, pushing aside distractions, and allowing you to perform at your best.

Now, let's consider a scenario where you might shank a shot or miss an easy one that, in the past, would have provoked frustration. You're no longer allowing it to bother you; instead, it's time to accept it and move on, back into the zone or flow. Tuning into your internal positive AutoThoughts and using self-hypnosis meditation is designed to unconsciously promote heightened present-moment awareness. Even when your mind starts to drift, these techniques gently bring you back to the present.

I've often said that thinking is like speaking to yourself, and words are magic to the receptive listener. It's fascinating how quickly a word or phrase can transform our reality. By combining these trigger words with visualization, you'll create a powerful training method that can be used both on and off the course.

Anchoring with Trigger Words

Being able to access a peak performance state on demand can make the difference between a good round and a great one. Anchoring with trigger words, especially when enhanced by self-hypnosis meditation, can help you tap into these optimal states whenever you need them.

Anchoring is a technique where you associate a specific physical action or word with a desired mental state. For example, you might press your thumb and forefinger together or say a specific word to yourself to trigger feelings of confidence, calm, or focus. By incorporating self-hypnosis, you can strengthen these anchors, making them more effective at bringing you into the right mind-set instantly.

To create an anchor, start by vividly imagining yourself in a peak performance state. Choose a simple action or word to associate with this state. I suggest selecting a word that provokes change or something out of the ordinary. For example, "Ferrari," "Ignite," and "Fire" are powerful, dynamic words. Alternatively, you could use a playful or unexpected word such as "ice cream," "pizza," or "bubblegum." As you say this word, associate it with being in peak awareness and performance mode. With repeated practice, this anchor will become a powerful tool you can rely on to access the mental state you need on the course.

Anchoring with Visualization

As I have already introduced in previous chapters, visualization is a cornerstone of mental conditioning in golf. It involves creating a vivid mental image of your desired outcome—whether it's the flight of the ball, the feel of a perfect swing, or the satisfaction of a successful putt. Enhance the effectiveness of visualization by making these mental images as vivid and impactful as possible. I would like to suggest the implantation of self-hypnosis medita-tion to enhance guided visualization.

Using self-hypnosis meditation, your mind becomes more receptive to suggestions and imagery, allowing you to create stronger mental blueprints for success. By regularly visualizing your perfect shot under hypnosis, you reinforce these images in your subconscious mind, making it easier to reproduce them in reality. Visualizing calmness and staying present allows this process to become automatic, without the need for overthinking.

During your self-hypnosis visualization sessions, immerse yourself fully in the experience. Feel the grip of the club, the tension in your muscles, and the wind on your face. See the ball's trajectory and hear the sound of a perfect strike. The more detailed and vivid your visualization, the more powerful the effect will be on your actual performance.

This is a powerful tool that can enhance every aspect of your golf game—from your pre-shot routine to your ability to stay present and focused under pressure. By integrating the techniques discussed in this chapter, you can develop a mental game that complements your physical skills, leading to more consistent and confident performances on the course.

As you practice these techniques, remember that progress takes time and consistent effort. The more you work with self-hypnosis meditation, the more natural and effective it will become. Over time, you'll find that these mental tools not only improve your golf game but also enhance your overall mindset, helping you approach challenges with calmness, focus, and resilience.

By adding these anchoring techniques to your mental toolbox, you expand your overall presence and control in the game. Golf, much like life, presents new challenges with every round, and your ability to adapt is key to sustaining peak performance. When you are more in tune, you can shift your perspective on a situation. Instead of viewing a challenging shot or a bad hole as a failure, reframe it as an opportunity to demonstrate your resilience and mental toughness. This shift in mindset can prevent negative emotions from derailing your performance and keep you anchored in the present moment.

You can use the techniques of *trigger words and visualization* separately, or you can combine them for even greater effect. When used together, they create a powerful synergy, enabling you to not only access your peak performance state more reliably but also to sustain it throughout the round. This combination strengthens your mental resilience, allowing you to recover quickly from setbacks and remain focused under pressure. By mastering these techniques, you will unlock a new level of consistency and confidence in your game, both on and off the course.

Long-Term Benefits

The benefits of these mental conditioning practices extend beyond just improving your golf game. As you become more proficient in using these techniques, you will notice a positive impact on other areas of your life. Your ability to remain calm under pressure, stay focused on the task at hand, and bounce back from setbacks enhances your overall well-being and effectiveness in various pursuits. These skills help you approach challenges in work, relationships, and personal growth with greater confidence and clarity, enabling you to manage stress more effectively and make better decisions under pressure.

The Scottie Scheffler Story

As an example of using mental conditional practices in life *and* golfing, let's consider the incident when pro golfer Scottie Scheffler (considered No. 1 golfer in the world) was arrested on May 17, 2024, at the scene of a traffic accident while he was driving to the Valhalla Golf Club for his tee time during PGA Championship week. He was booked on serious charges, fingerprinted, and placed in a holding cell. He said he was never angry, but he was in shock. "I was shaking the whole time. I was shaking for like an hour," he said. "It was definitely a new feeling for me." After he was released on his own recognizance, Scheffler was picked up by the golf club owner and taken to the golf club. He arrived to play on the 10th tee. He said later in an interview: "It probably took a few holes to feel normal. Obviously, I didn't have my normal warm-up, and I usually stick to my routine, and I'm a big routine guy, especially when it comes to my preparation," he said. "It was kind of nice just to be out there inside the ropes competing. It's one of my favorite things in the world to do."

Scheffler gained the most help from being back in his comfort zone. The experience could have easily put him into a state of shock and fear, which might have made playing golf a huge challenge. To deal with his distracted state, Scheffler said, "I did my best to control my mind, control my breathing. Basically, just calm down so I could come out here and try and play golf." He ended up turning in a classic Scheffler performance, despite his rattling experience. Less than two weeks later, all charges against Scottie Scheffler were dismissed.

By anchoring yourself in positive mental states, using visualization to create a clear mental blueprint, and expanding your mental toolbox with techniques like progressive relaxation, breath control, and emotional reframing, you set yourself up for success both on and off the course. Whether you are negotiating a deal in the boardroom, having a tough conversation with a loved one, or navigating unforeseen challenges in your personal life, these mental techniques equip you with the composure, presence, and resilience to handle any situation.

The ripple effect of this mindset conditioning transforms your overall quality of life. You will experience increased self-awareness, emotional intelligence, and a sense of inner control that helps you thrive in high-stress environments. Furthermore, the ability to shift your mindset on demand empowers you to consistently operate from a place of strength and positivity, allowing you to grow through challenges rather than be hindered by them.

Remember, these practices require time and patience, but the rewards are well worth the effort. As you consistently apply these tools, you will find that setbacks no longer define your outcomes, and obstacles become opportunities for growth. The more you invest in your mental conditioning, the more you will see your game—and your life—elevate to new heights, creating lasting changes in your confidence, focus, and overall success.

Mindsetcaddie Reset

> **Mindfulness:** Cultivating mindfulness allows you to quickly refocus and stay present after a setback, ensuring that distractions and negative thoughts don't disrupt your performance. This skill is essential for maintaining consistency and resilience, particularly in high-pressure situations.

> **Anchoring:** Using anchoring with trigger words and visualization is a powerful method to quickly access and sustain a peak performance state of mind. These techniques help establish a mental routine that becomes automatic under pressure, enabling you to remain calm, focused, and confident during challenging moments on the course.

> **Be Present:** Swiftly shifting your attention back to the present moment after a mistake prevents distractions from affecting your performance. Quick recovery is crucial for maintaining composure and consistency, especially in difficult situations. This can also be used to maintain being present and in the flow.

Mindsetcaddie Redirect

❯ Create and practice an anchoring technique with a trigger word. Choose a specific word, such as "Ignite" or "Focus," that you can associate with a peak performance state. Make it unique to you with meaning Think of a word that has a powerful memory of happiness or success. If could be a reminder of an accomplishment or even a celebration. It should be a word that empowers you with an emotion of positive thoughts. Practice saying this word while visualizing yourself playing at your best—calm, confident, and fully present. Repeat this exercise regularly, both on and off the course, to build a mental anchor that you can rely on during high-pressure moments to regain focus and stay in the zone.

❯ Incorporate mindful visualizations into your pre-shot routine. Before each shot, take a moment to visualize your ideal outcome in vivid detail, including the ball's flight and your confident swing. Combine this visualization with deep breathing to calm your mind and reinforce mental clarity. By making this part of your pre-shot routine, you enhance your focus and prepare your mind to perform automatically, even under pressure.

❯ As a reinforcement tool, you can now listen to Day Eight in the audio program in my app. I will guide you through the breathing and meditation exercise to promote calmness, awareness, and guided thought, adding elements based on this chapter.

TRAINING CONSISTENCY

The power of resilience lies in
rising every time we fall!

CONSISTENCY PLAYS a critical role in golf, creating a mental environment where positive thoughts, confidence, and the unwavering belief that you can win become your default setting. This consistent practice establishes a zone of comfort, presence, and readiness, which is essential for peak performance on the course.

When golfers are "in the zone," they are mentally in that place of comfort and readiness. They achieve this by consistently repeating the thoughts, visualizations, and techniques that engrain the belief they can succeed. This repetition solidifies their commitment to their goals, turning their desires into reality and fostering an unshakable belief in their ability to win.

Your commitment to consistency is crucial to developing your talent and achieving success. It's not just about repeating actions but also about cultivating a constancy of habits that reinforce the belief in yourself, your ability to win, and your confidence in every aspect of your game. The more you reinforce these beliefs through repetition, the more they become ingrained in your mindset, driving your success on the course.

You can't just have one good round and say, "I've got this covered." Every day brings new opportunities, challenges, and potential growth. To truly excel, you must engage in consistent daily practice that trains your brain to respond automatically with confidence and belief in your abilities. This ongoing mental conditioning is what keeps you sharp, resilient, and ready to perform at your best, no matter what the day throws at you.

I recently had a conversation with two of my golf clients. Both have experienced my programs during in-person coaching to continue their mindset skills development. In addition, they have access to all of the premium programs in my app, which gives them a choice to select a topic that resonates with them to focus on in their mindset training. One of them told me he initially used the app enthusiastically for about a week but then admitted to slacking off and somewhat reverting to old negative habits. The other client smiled and humbly shared that he logged in daily and was sleeping better, experiencing less stress, and seeing consistent improvement in his game—attributing the progress to the consistency of the routine.

I have worked with both collegiate and professional golfers to help them enter the zone, where peak performance is possible. This state is often referred to as being "in the flow." When you're in the zone, confidence is at its peak and you have laser-like focus. You are completely absorbed in the task at hand, free from distractions. However, achieving this flow and maintaining the belief that you can win is impossible without the right mindset.

The key to getting into the zone lies in becoming comfortable with your task through conscious, deliberate repetition. When a task becomes second nature, it becomes automatic—a state of true comfort. But beyond just being comfortable with the task, it's essential to cultivate a constant belief in your ability to succeed, in your skills, and in your strategy. When you add trust and the belief that you can win to this equation, your mindset shifts into overdrive, helping you achieve the outcomes you know are possible.

Research shows that mental training is highly effective in achieving a flow state. Studies involving golfers have revealed that those who practice mental training are better able to enter the zone. The more they engage in mental training, the better they perform, free from external and internal distractions, such as negative thoughts or emotions. This mental training not only enhances focus, it also deeply engrains the belief that winning is within their grasp, that their skills are reliable, and that every aspect of their game is solid.

One such study in *Sport and Exercise Psychology Review* reveals a glimpse into emotions and performance. M.S. Allen observed that when athletes performed below their usual standard, they felt angry and dejected. Poor performance almost always resulted in negative emotions, and good performance resulted in a heightened sense of control and ability to cope with problems.

This is a crucial point, because many studies show that the athlete's sense of control is associated with their performance. In other words, an athlete who strongly believes in their own personal ability (control) usually performs better than an athlete who attributes their performance to luck or to their opponent's abilities. When an athlete does well but chooses to think of their success as due to a lucky day or an opponent's mistake, their emotions remain primarily negative. They experience more anxiety, and their overall performance outcomes are lower. Greater skill level and better overall performance are associated with athlete's who perceive themselves to be in control of their own outcomes.

Studies show that over time, emotions and performance have a dynamic and reciprocal effect upon each other. During a competition, the range of emotional states and performance outcomes can shift and change. Athletes may perceive themselves to have more control in some aspects of the game than in others. Tracking and noticing the interplay of these factors and the changes over time is crucial to success, especially in competitions that last a long time, such as golf.

Just as you've heard the saying, "Keep saying it and you will start believing it," this principle holds true in golf as well. Repetition is a time-tested method for success, whether in improving your swing, staying focused, or reinforcing positive beliefs, including the belief that you can and will win. Repeatedly telling yourself that you have what it takes builds a foundation of self-belief that supports every shot you make.

Often, we extend this encouragement to others—friends, family, teammates—but forget to apply it to ourselves. We must remember to be our own cheerleaders, repeating positive affirmations until they become natural, helping us stay in the zone and maintain the belief in our ability to win during our game. This consistent self-encouragement builds a resilient mindset that believes in winning, even when facing adversity.

The essence of mastering your mindset in golf is repetition. This process involves reinforcing positive thoughts, practicing visualization, and repeating techniques until they become second nature. Once these elements are deeply ingrained, including the belief that you are a winner, you can provide yourself with the same support you've given to others throughout your life. A consistent habit of believing in yourself, in your skills, and in your strategy is what will set you apart on the course.

Just as we encourage others to stay positive and focused, we need to apply the same strategies to ourselves. Repeating these positive thoughts, visualizing success, and affirming your belief in your ability to win are key to maintaining and shifting your mindset for long-term success. Trusting in your mind, in your ability to win, and in every aspect of your game produces trust in your talent, leading to greater consistency and success.

To make lasting changes to your golf mindset, repetition must become part of your lifestyle and identity. Repeating what you've learned about relaxation, trust, and believing in your potential helps program your mindset for peak performance and success. But more than that, you must consistently practice the habit of believing in yourself, in your capacity to win, and in every element of your game—from your swing to your mental approach.

Overcoming Common Pitfalls

It's easy to start strong with a new routine but then let it slip as life gets busy. Here are some tips to maintain consistency:

> **Set Small, Achievable Goals**: Break down your practice into manageable steps to avoid feeling overwhelmed. Make *Leverage Your Mindset* training part of your daily practice. Whether five or fifteen minutes, setting achievable goals is imperative to daily commitment.

> **Accountability**: No one is responsible for your actions but you. Hold yourself accountable. Share your goals with a friend, coach, or fellow golfer who can help keep you on track.

> **Celebrate Small Wins**: Recognize and celebrate your progress, no matter how small, to keep your motivation high. Are you less stressed? Do you have fewer swing thoughts? Are you enjoying the game more? Are you less critical of where the ball lands? When you bank your small wins, you accumulate strong feelings of confidence and belief.

Your mind is a powerful tool that doesn't want to let you down. When you repeat something often enough, you start to believe it, respond to it, and act on it. This concept works both positively and negatively; if you repeatedly tell yourself you can't do something, your mind will accept that as truth and act accordingly. Conversely, if you engrain the belief that you can win, your mind will work to make that belief a reality. Consistent belief in your abilities across all aspects of the game—mental, physical, and strategic—cements the foundation for sustained peak performance.

Repetition

The subconscious mind is particularly susceptible to repetition, as it constantly absorbs the messages you feed it. This is why the thoughts you allow to circulate in your mind are so powerful. When you consciously choose to focus on constructive AutoThoughts, you reinforce a mindset geared toward growth, resilience, and success. Whether it's on the golf course, in your career, or in your personal relationships, the beliefs you repeat become the blueprint for your actions and ultimately shape your outcomes. When you embrace a positive internal dialogue, your actions will naturally align with that narrative, propelling you toward your goals with greater confidence and focus.

The most successful people understand that consistent reinforcement of positive beliefs, goals, and behaviors creates lasting change.

Whether you're a golfer looking to improve your mental game, a sales professional seeking to grow your business, or a leader aiming to inspire your team, repetition is key to functioning at peak performance. The most successful individuals across any field understand that the consistent reinforcement of positive beliefs, goals, and behaviors is what creates lasting change. Your reality is shaped by what you believe, and what you believe is influenced by what you repeat. Therefore, be intentional about repeating the right thoughts, actions, and beliefs to shape your game and mindset for success.

This process of mental conditioning doesn't happen overnight, but over time, the repetition of empowering beliefs rewires your brain to default toward positive outcomes. The more you consciously engage in repeating positive affirmations and visualizing success, the more natural it becomes to operate from a place of optimism and confidence. In doing so, you unlock the ability to sustain peak performance, not only when things are going well, but also in moments of adversity, when your resilience and belief system truly shine.

MindsetCaddie Reset

> **Consistency Is Key to Success:** Achieving and maintaining peak performance in golf requires consistent daily practice, not just a few good rounds. Repetition of positive thoughts, visualizations, and techniques

ingrains confidence and the belief that you can win, making them an integral part of your mindset.

> **The Power of Routine:** Establishing a regular mental conditioning routine—whether through visualization, affirmations, or reflective journaling—helps reinforce your belief in yourself and your abilities. Consistent routines are crucial for staying in the zone, improving performance, and building resilience against challenges.

> **Belief Shapes Reality:** Your mindset is shaped by what you repeatedly tell yourself. By consistently practicing positive affirmations and mental exercises, you train your mind to believe in your ability to win, which in turn influences your actions and results on the course.

MindsetCaddie Redirect

> Develop resilience by embracing setbacks as growth opportunities. When faced with a setback during practice or a round, use it as a moment to reinforce resilience. Instead of reacting negatively, pause and reflect on what you can learn from the situation. Regularly repeating this process of turning challenges into learning opportunities will train your mind to respond with resilience. Over time, this habit strengthens your mental toughness, allowing you to bounce back quickly and maintain

focus, confidence, and belief in your ability to succeed under any circumstances. Make consistency a daily practice.

> Set small, achievable goals, and celebrate wins regularly. Break down your mental training and performance improvement into small, actionable steps that you can practice consistently. After each practice or round of golf, reflect on your progress and celebrate even the smallest wins, such as staying calm after a bad shot or successfully using a visualization technique. These small celebrations will boost your confidence and motivation, reinforcing the belief that you are capable of consistent improvement and success.

> As a reinforcement tool, you can now listen to Day Nine in the audio program in my app. I will guide you through the breathing and meditation exercise to promote calmness, awareness, and guided thought, adding elements based on this chapter.

REWRITING YOUR MENTAL SOFTWARE

Your potential is limitless—only
your beliefs hold you back.

AT SOME POINT of your life, someone has likely told you to relax, don't overthink, or that you just need to focus better. While these might be valid suggestions, they're often just commands—simple statements that don't provide the tools or techniques needed to actually improve. That's where this book and my content come in. My goal is to go beyond the "commands" or the "I wants" and equip you with the tools to become a better golfer and a better version of yourself. From the first line of this book, we've been working on updating your internal operating system with a plan of action.

We all constantly set goals, dreams, and thoughts in our minds, whether we consciously acknowledge it or not. We update this mental list all the time, often in ways that don't support us. The challenge is that much of this updating happens unconsciously, leading to habits and beliefs that may sabotage our success on the course.

Golfers have told me things such as, "Oh, I could never stay calm during a high-stakes putt." Guess what just happened? That golfer has reinforced a long-standing belief on their mental list. Whenever I hear something like that, I'm tempted to say, "You're right. You can't. You just made sure of that. What else are you determined not to be able to do?" While this may sound harsh, it highlights the importance of recognizing the clutter on our mental lists—the destructive AutoThoughts that hold us back—and flipping the script to turn our mental lists into gold.

Today, I want you to become aware of the clutter on your default mental list—the outdated app you've been feeding your mind, including the negative feelings, assumptions, and messages that come up automatically. As a golfer, this might sound like:

> "I always choke under pressure."

> "I'm never going to fix my slice."

> "I can't compete with the other players."

These are the bits of mental junk cluttering your default list. But here's the good news: you can rewrite them into positive affirmations that support your growth and success. For example:

> "I thrive under pressure."

> "I am constantly improving my swing."

> "I am a strong competitor who can hold my own."

The goal is to use your negative thoughts as a starting point to create positive affirmations. Begin today to create actual results that can serve as evidence to support these constructive beliefs. For instance, if your default thought is, *I'm unlucky on the course,* notice it, and then transform it into something like, *I'm grateful for the opportunities and successes I encounter on the course every golf day.* As you reinforce this new belief, you will start to notice the tangible opportunities that come your way and be more likely to act on them.

But it's not enough to just think about these changes; you need to actively write them out. Why? Because when you write, you engage with your thoughts on a deeper level, bringing clarity and focus to your intentions. Writing serves as a powerful tool to reinforce the new pathways you're creating in your mind. It's the difference between vaguely wanting something—and declaring it with conviction.

Become the Programmer of Your New Mental Software

Think of yourself as the programmer of your new mental software. Your mind is like a computer, and the thoughts, beliefs, and habits you've developed are the code that runs it. If the code is full of bugs—negative thoughts, doubts, and outdated beliefs—your mental software won't run efficiently. It's time to debug your mental software and write a new script that supports your goals and aspirations.

Start by identifying the "bugs" in your mental code—those automatic negative thoughts, self-doubts, and limiting beliefs that hold you back. Once you recognize these patterns, you can replace them with positive affirmations, empowering beliefs, and mental techniques that reinforce success. This process requires consistent effort, much like programming: you must deliberately input the new, positive code and repeat it until it becomes embedded in your mental framework.

As the programmer, you have full control. You can customize your mental operating system to work in alignment with your goals by focusing on growth, confidence, and resilience. Just like any well-written software, your mental code requires regular updates. Continually assess your mindset, fine-tune your thoughts, and adapt your beliefs to reflect your evolving aspirations.

With each mental update, you will notice greater clarity, more effective decision-making, and a stronger ability to overcome challenges, both on and off the course. By becoming the active programmer of your mind, you unlock new levels of performance and potential.

We Have Been Working On

1. **Identifying the Bugs:** Start by identifying the negative thoughts and beliefs holding you back. What are the recurring themes in your self-talk that undermine your confidence and performance?

2. **Rewriting the Code:** For each negative thought, write out a positive affirmation that directly counters it. Be specific and intentional. For example, if you often think, *I'm terrible at putting under pressure,* rewrite it as, *I excel at putting under pressure because I stay calm and focused.*

3. **Creating a Script:** Once you've rewritten your negative thoughts into positive affirmations, create a script that you can review daily. This script should include statements that enforce your intentions, direction, and focus on the present moment. Write it out by hand, as this can help reinforce the new pathways in your brain.

4. **Practicing Daily:** Review your script every day, preferably in the morning and before you go to bed. As you read through it, visualize yourself embodying these beliefs on the course. The more you practice, the more these affirmations will become ingrained in your mindset, transforming your mental game. This is exactly what

I encourage you to do—daily practice of relaxation and visualization to update your internal operating system.

5. **Reinforcing with Action:** It's important to back up your script with actions that align with your new beliefs. For example, if your script includes, "I am improving my swing," make sure you're putting in the practice to refine your technique. Actions reinforce beliefs, creating a powerful feedback loop that drives success.

Updating Your Mental Script

Writing out your new mental script is crucial because it takes your abstract thoughts and makes them tangible. It's a commitment to yourself, a declaration that you are in control of your mental game. When you write, you are not just thinking about what you want to achieve—you are actively programming your mind to manifest those desires into reality.

Writing helps you focus on the present moment. By committing your intentions to paper, you anchor yourself in the now, reducing the likelihood of being distracted by past mistakes or future worries. This present-moment awareness is key to performing your best on the course, where staying in the moment can make all the difference between a good shot and a great one.

Having a coach by our side all the time isn't practical. At some point, you're left with only your personal resources—you're on your own. That's why it's essential to trust the most powerful coach in the world: yourself!

You already have the power within you to achieve your goals on the course. Sure, I can guide you at key points along the way, but I can't hit the ball for you, make the putt, or keep your focus sharp under pressure. The only person who has that power is you. And while I don't have a magic wand to make you a better golfer, you do—it's the instructions you feed your mindset.

You are now your own coach. So, here's a coaching challenge: Just like no one can make you feel bad about yourself without your permission, no one can make you feel good about yourself without your permission either. Which way is it going to go? Which permission will you give?

Imagine that you are coaching someone just like you. Would you tell that person, "You can't do it. Don't even try. This is a waste of time"? Of course not! You'd be invested in that person's success and would do and say everything you could to create positive results. Yet, as our own coaches, we are often guilty of sabotaging our success with our words, thoughts, and beliefs—even before we begin.

You are in charge here. I can guide you, but ultimately, you are the driver on your journey. You have control over your destiny on the course, and no one else can take that control from you without your permission.

If you truly want to achieve something in golf, you must believe that you can. That belief has to be stronger than any doubt that might have previously existed. You must be willing to be your own coach, your strongest supporter, and your biggest cheerleader. Build a relationship based on trust—with yourself. Using the techniques I've shared with you, I know you can unlock the power within yourself and become the best golfer you can be.

Not Yesterday, Not Tomorrow, but Today!

The big questions for you today and for every day moving forward:

> ❯ What do you want your brain, your mindset to do?

> ❯ What realities do you want to manifest on the course?

> ❯ What experiences do you want to lead yourself toward?

> ❯ What doors do you want to open for you?

Use today to gain real clarity with these questions, and start collecting victories with your answers. When you achieve those victories, be sure to reinforce them. Celebrate your successes. Reward yourself. Let positive reinforcement increase your focus on what you want. Soon, without even thinking about it, you'll find that you're naturally acting on the positive items on your list, both on and off the course.

The process of transforming your mental game isn't about simply wanting to be better, it's about actively updating your internal operating system to support your success. Every time you replace a negative thought with a positive one, you're rewriting your mental game. And just like in golf, where practice creates muscle memory, the more you practice positive reinforcement, it becomes mind memory.

By continually updating and reinforcing your mental app, you'll find that your golf game—and your life—begins to align more closely with your goals and desires. The power is in your hands, or more accurately, in your mind. It's time to take control, rewrite your mental game, and start winning.

MindsetCaddie Reset

> **Your Mindset Is Your Best Coach:** While external coaches can guide and refine your skills, the most powerful coach you have is yourself. Trust in your own ability to guide your mental game, reinforcing positive beliefs and actions that align with your goals on the course.

> **Reprogram Your Mental Software:** Just as you would debug and update software, you must actively rewrite the negative thoughts and beliefs that hold you back. By creating a daily script of positive affirmations and

practicing them consistently, you program your mind for success in golf and beyond.

> **The Power of Writing and Reinforcement:** Writing out your intentions and beliefs is a crucial step in making them real and actionable. By committing your goals to paper and regularly reinforcing them with positive actions, you align your mindset with your desired outcomes, making success more attainable and sustainable.

MindsetCaddie Redirect

> Identify and replace limiting beliefs. Start by identifying one limiting belief that holds you back, such as "I always choke under pressure." Once identified, replace it with a positive affirmation like, "I thrive under pressure." Write this affirmation down and repeat it daily. By reinforcing this positive belief regularly, you reprogram your mindset for success, helping you overcome the mental barriers that have previously hindered your performance.

> Commit to being your own coach. Challenge yourself to consciously choose the permission you give: Will you allow yourself to feel empowered or defeated? Take a moment to imagine you are coaching someone exactly like you. Would you tell the person, "You can't do it,"

or discourage them from trying? Of course not! You'd be the person's biggest supporter, guiding the individual toward success. So, treat yourself the same way. Speak, think, and believe in your potential, and take actions that reflect the success you want to create. Write down one supportive thought you will repeat to yourself daily, and commit to it.

❯ As a reinforcement tool, you can now listen to Day Ten in the audio program in my app. I will guide you through the breathing and meditation exercise to promote calmness, awareness, and guided thought, adding elements based on this chapter.

DAY ELEVEN

INTERNAL OPERATING
SYSTEM UPDATE

To elevate your game, you must first upgrade
your internal operating system—refresh your
mindset, clear out self-doubt, and install focus
and resilience for success on every swing.

UP UNTIL NOW, we've been preparing your mind, helping you build awareness through relaxation techniques, gratitude
practices, and setting aside time dedicated to honing your mental
game. Now it's time to start updating your mental software—a
process that has been a game-changer for many of my clients,
enabling them to unlock new levels of performance, focus, and
success on the golf course.

If you're serious about improving your golf game, this chapter
will be especially valuable. By fully engaging with the strategies
laid out here, you won't just enhance your own ability to reach
your golfing goals—you'll also create a mindset that consistently supports peak performance. Incorporating these mental

techniques into your routine can lead to breakthroughs in your game that you may not have thought possible.

Golfers, like top professionals in any field, understand the importance of continuous improvement. Even the best players are always looking for ways to fine-tune their swing, sharpen their focus, and elevate their strategy. Just as a business updates its systems to stay competitive, you need to regularly refresh your mental approach to keep your game sharp. Your mindset is like an app that's always running in the background—it never stops. However, it operates based on the most recent and dominant instructions it has received—specifically, your most consistent thoughts, beliefs, and emotions.

To keep performing at your best, it's crucial to ensure that the mental software guiding your game is current and aligned with your goals. Outdated beliefs, old habits, and negative thoughts can hold you back and prevent you from playing your best. This chapter is all about recognizing those outdated mental patterns and replacing them with a mindset that supports the golfer you aspire to be.

Crafting Your Golfer's Software

To effectively update your mental software, you need a clear and specific code for success. Think of this code as your personal game plan—a detailed guide that outlines your goals, intentions, and the mindset you want to cultivate. Just as you wouldn't build a golf course without a solid design, you shouldn't approach your game without a mental game plan.

Creating this code involves more than just thinking about what you want; it requires actively writing it down. This written code becomes your guide, one that you can refer to and refine regularly. Writing things down is a powerful way to bring clarity and focus to your intentions. It's a process of self-discovery that helps you identify what truly matters in your golf game.

Step-by-Step Guide to Crafting Your Software

Step 1: Set Aside Time

Dedicate a specific time each day, even just 10 minutes, to write down your thoughts, goals, and affirmations. Consistency is key—make this a non-negotiable part of your daily routine.

Step 2: Create a Dedicated Space

Use the space provided at the end of this book labeled for Notes, a specific journal, or a digital document exclusively for your mental game plan. This helps maintain focus and allows you to track your progress over time.

Step 3: Start with Gratitude

Begin each session by writing down one or two things you're grateful for. This practice sets a positive tone and primes your mind for constructive thinking.

Step 4: Write in the Present Tense

Frame your goals and affirmations as if they are already happening. For example, instead of writing "I will stay calm under pressure," write, "I am calm under pressure." This reinforces the belief that these qualities are already part of who you are.

Step 5: Visualize as You Write

As you write, take a moment to visualize yourself achieving what you're writing about. Imagine the sights, sounds, and feelings associated with your success. This deepens the connection between your mental blueprint and your real-world performance.

For example:

January 1

Grateful

I am grateful for the opportunities that I have been given. I am grateful for the lessons learned from both successes and failures, shaping my journey forward.

Goals and Affirmations

I am accepting constructive AutoThoughts throughout my day today, rejecting all destructive AutoThoughts.

I am confident and grounded in self-assurance rather than arrogance.

Visualization

Tomorrow when I'm playing a round, I see myself walking onto the tee box and looking down the fairway toward the green. I see the flag at the hole slightly waving in the wind. The club in my hand, like a glove. Looking at the small, white dimpled ball at my feet, I take my stance and adjust my shoulders. Now I see me swinging the club and the ball sailing down the fairway toward the hole and landing and rolling for a bit, exactly where I aimed it to go.

Why Writing Matters

Writing down your goals and thoughts is more than just a simple exercise; it's a proven method for solidifying your intentions and making them more real. Research shows that when goals are written down, they are significantly more likely to be achieved. Writing engages different parts of your brain, reinforcing your thoughts and making them stronger and more consistent. This practice also helps you see your potential more clearly and focus on what you want to accomplish on the course.

The act of writing serves as a bridge between your conscious intentions and your subconscious mind. By putting your goals on paper, you are effectively programming your brain to recognize opportunities, focus on key objectives, and dismiss distractions. This is particularly important in golf, where mental focus can make the difference between a great shot and a missed opportunity.

Writing things down allows you to track your progress over time. It gives you a tangible record of your growth, enabling you to see how far you've come and what areas still need work. This ongoing reflection is vital for maintaining motivation and keeping your mental game strong.

Designing Your Mental Software Code

Your mental software code should be a living document—a written list that evolves as you grow and change. This list should capture your aspirations, both on and off the course, and serve as a code for how you want to approach your game. Whether it's building confidence, mastering a new skill, or refining your mental approach under pressure, your plan should include positive affirmations stated in the present tense, as if you've already achieved them. For example:

> ❯ "I am calm and focused on every shot."
> ❯ "I am consistently making solid contact with the ball."
> ❯ "I excel in high-pressure situations."
> ❯ "I trust my swing and play with confidence."
> ❯ "I am resilient and bounce back quickly from setbacks."
> ❯ "I am in control of my emotions, maintaining a positive attitude throughout my round."
> ❯ "I am visualizing success before every shot and follow through with precision."
> ❯ "I am enjoying the game and embracing every challenge as an opportunity to grow."

These affirmations help create a mental framework that supports your goals and reinforces the belief that you can achieve them. The more you repeat these positive statements, the more they become ingrained in your subconscious, guiding your actions and decisions on the course.

Daily Practice for Lasting Change

Consistency is key to making these mental changes stick. Review your mental code every day, preferably before heading to the course, and again as you reflect on your day. The more you engage with your written code, the more it becomes embedded in your subconscious, guiding your actions and decisions without you even realizing it.

This daily practice not only helps reinforce your goals but also provides an opportunity to reflect on your progress and make adjustments as needed. It's a chance to celebrate small victories, learn from setbacks, and continue refining your mental game.

Incorporate this practice into your daily routine, just like you would a physical workout or a practice session. Dedicate a few minutes each day to review your goals, visualize your success, and mentally prepare for the challenges ahead. Over time, this mental conditioning will become second nature, giving you a distinct advantage on the course.

Updating Your Mental Software Code

As you continue to refine your mental software code, you'll notice that certain thoughts, beliefs, and habits no longer serve you. This is your opportunity to update your mental software—replacing outdated mental patterns with new, empowering ones. By regularly *reviewing and updating your game plan, you ensure that your mindset is always aligned with your goals.*

Remember, your mind is your most powerful tool on the course. By taking the time to consciously update and refine your mental software, you're setting yourself up for success. Your mental game plan is not just a list of goals—it's a dynamic, living document that evolves with you, helping you become the golfer you aspire to be.

Think of your mental game plan as a constantly evolving strategy. As you achieve certain goals or encounter new challenges, adjust your plan accordingly. This flexibility ensures that your mindset remains sharp and responsive to whatever the game throws your way.

Waking Hypnosis

If you've been diligently following the action activities within MindsetCaddie Resets and Redirects, let me offer some clarity: with each exercise and example that resonates with you, you're engaging in a form of self-hypnosis called *Waking Hypnosis.* This is a powerful process where, even though you're fully awake and alert, you're training your subconscious mind through focused thoughts, emotions, and actions.

In simple terms, Waking Hypnosis is hypnosis without the whole relaxation aspect. I have always defined it as the *power of suggestion.* Waking hypnosis guides you consciously and unconsciously, allowing you to direct your attention toward specific ideas or beliefs, which then sink into your subconscious mind. This can happen during moments when you're highly engaged in an activity or deeply resonating with a thought. For instance, you could be in a casual conversation with a friend about your favorite pizza and end up ordering it that same day. Or you might briefly see a picture, ad, or commercial, and it imprints a positive intention to purchase a product.

The point is, the more you embrace positive self-talk, visualizations, and belief in yourself, the more you're in a state of unconscious waking hypnosis. When you do this regularly, these thoughts reinforce new mental patterns, replacing old, unhelpful ones. You are essentially *reprogramming* your mind by choosing which thoughts to believe and act upon, creating new automatic behaviors that align with your goals.

The more you practice, the stronger these new neural pathways become, helping you stay calm, confident, and focused in high-pressure situations. This is the essence of waking hypnosis—an intentional, self-directed way to harness the power of your mind, consciously and unconsciously, to create the results you desire.

Your Updated Internal Software

As you move forward, keep in mind that your mindset is your most valuable caddie. Just as a caddie helps you navigate the physical challenges of the course, your mindset guides you through the mental challenges. By regularly updating your mental software, you're equipping yourself with the tools to handle any situation on the course with confidence and composure.

Take the time each day to review your mental software code, write down your goals, and reinforce the positive beliefs that will help you succeed. This practice will not only improve your performance on the course but also enhance your overall well-being and resilience in life.

Your mindset is the foundation of your success in golf. By treating it as an ever-evolving tool, you can continuously refine your approach, overcome challenges, and achieve the goals you've set for yourself. The power is in your hands—or more accurately, in your mind. Now it's time to take control, rewrite your mental game, and start winning.

This holistic approach to updating your mental game empowers you to reach new heights in your golfing journey. It's about more than just hitting the ball well—it's about cultivating a mindset that supports excellence, resilience, and joy in the game. Embrace this process, and you'll find that not only does your golf game improve, but so does your overall experience of the sport.

Mindsetcaddie Reset

> **Consistently Update Your Mental Software:** Your mindset is like an app that needs regular updates to stay aligned with your goals. By consistently reviewing and refining your mental game plan, you ensure that your thoughts, beliefs, and habits support your growth as a golfer.

> **The Power of Writing and Visualization:** Writing down your goals and affirmations in the present tense helps solidify your intentions and makes them more achievable. Coupled with visualization, this practice creates a strong mental framework that guides your actions and decisions on the course.

> **Treat Your Mindset as a Dynamic Tool:** Your mental game plan should be a living document that evolves as you progress in your golfing journey. Regularly updating this plan ensures that your mindset remains sharp, responsive, and aligned with the challenges and opportunities you face on the course.

Mindsetcaddie Redirect

> Write down a list of powerful "I am" statements that reflect the qualities and beliefs you want to cultivate in yourself. For example, "I am confident under pressure," "I am constantly improving my game," or, "I am resilient in the face of challenges." Repeat these affirmations daily, especially before practice or competition, to reinforce your mental resilience and belief in your abilities.

> At the end of each day, set aside time to reflect on how your "I am" statements have impacted your mindset and performance. Write down any improvements you've noticed or areas where your new beliefs have helped you overcome challenges. This reflection will help reinforce the positive mental changes and keep you motivated to continue using the affirmations regularly.

> As a reinforcement tool, you can now listen to Day Eleven in the audio program in my app. I will guide you through the breathing and meditation exercise to promote calmness, awareness, and guided thought, adding elements based on this chapter.

DAY TWELVE

RANGE FINDER IN
YOUR MIND

Challenge the status quo of your
beliefs. Growth is on the other side.

IN MY FIRST BOOK, *Leverage Your Mindset,* I introduce the idea of using your mindset as a powerful tool to shape
your reality. Leading up to this chapter, we explored how your
thoughts, beliefs, and attitudes influence every aspect of your life,
from your relationships to your career.

Now it's time to revisit those principles and take them to the
golf course where the power of your mindset can be the difference
between a good round and a great one. The ability to control your
thoughts, manage your emotions, and maintain focus under pressure is what separates the champions from the rest.

Today, we're going to dive deeper into this concept by applying the principles of the *Mindset Magnet*—a tool that helps you
align your mental game with your physical skills to achieve peak

performance. For the purpose of this book, I am rebranding this concept as the *Range Finder in Your Mind*.

A range finder in golf is a device used to measure the distance from your current position to a specific target on the course, such as the flagstick, a hazard, or a point on the fairway. Similarly, the range finder in your mind acts like a GPS for your thoughts, constantly guiding you toward your best self and your best outcomes, no matter the challenges you face on the course. It ensures that your mental app is always functioning at its peak, maximizing your potential so you can achieve excellence in every round.

But using the range finder in your mind isn't just a one-time effort, it's a way of life. It's a mindset that continually attracts and manifests what you want to be, have, and do, guiding you closer to your goals with every minute you spend on the green. Every successful golfer has a range finder that pulls them toward victory; and with the right approach, you can develop one too.

To help you fully grasp and utilize this concept, let's look at how you might apply it in a real golf scenario.

Practical Example

Imagine you're on the 15th hole of a challenging course. The wind has picked up, and you're standing over the ball, trying to decide between a 7-iron or a 6-iron for an approach shot to the green. Here's where the range finder in your mind becomes invaluable. Just as you would use a physical range finder to measure the distance and consider the environmental factors, you now tap into your *mental range finder.*

First, you take a deep breath, clearing your mind of any doubts or distractions. Then, you visualize the shot—seeing the ball's trajectory and imagining the perfect landing on the green. Your mental range finder helps you assess not just the physical distance, but also your confidence level, your focus, and your commitment to the shot. Trusting in your process, you choose the club with certainty, execute the shot, and watch as the ball lands exactly where you envisioned.

This is the power of the range finder in your mind: it guides your thoughts, emotions, and decisions, ensuring they align with your best outcomes. Every time you face a tough decision or feel your confidence wavering, remember to use your mental range finder to reset, refocus, and proceed with clarity and purpose.

Relating to Common Golf Experiences

Many golfers experience frustration, self-doubt, or decision paralysis during a round. The range finder in your mind can help navigate these mental challenges by keeping you focused on your target and committed to your decisions. When you feel the pressure mounting, whether it's from a difficult lie, an important match, or just the weight of expectations, your mental range finder acts as your compass. It directs your thoughts away from negativity and toward the actions that will bring you success. This tool isn't just for the good shots; it's crucial when things aren't going perfectly. By keeping your mind aligned with your goals, you maintain your composure and improve your performance, even under pressure.

U.S. Open champion Bryson DeChambeau made a video that explained in great analytical detail how to use a ruler to mark 10-foot, 20-foot, and 30-foot distances and use those to determine how hard to hit the putts. He explains in the video that as he practices those 10-footer, 20-footer, or 30-footer putts, all he's doing is referencing his foot for the exact spot where the putter head should be. Then, over the course of time, repeated practice ingrains that measurement into a feel until he can hit a 10-footer perfectly every single time. He says, "For me, that's what helps me control my speed the best and allows me to perform at the highest level."

Transitioning from Physical to Mental Tools

Golfers, like DeChambeau, are accustomed to using physical range finders to calculate distances and plan their shots. Think of the range finder in your mind as an extension of that tool—but one that measures mental distances instead of physical ones. Just as you wouldn't take a shot without knowing the distance, you shouldn't make decisions on the course without first consulting your mental range finder. This internal guide helps you assess your mental state, focus on your target, and execute your plan with confidence. By drawing a direct parallel between these two tools, you can better understand how to use your mental range finder to its full potential.

To create and strengthen your range finder, you need to master three simple yet powerful principles: *Relax, Trust,* and *Repeat.* These principles have been woven throughout this book, and now it's time to truly master them. The nine insights I'm about to share will help you magnetize your mindset and elevate your game.

RELAX:
Three Insights to Magnetize Mindset with Relaxation

Insight One:
Focus on Why You're Relaxing

Relaxation isn't just about feeling good, it's about preparing your mind for peak performance. When you relax, you clear your mind of distractions, stress, and negative thoughts, allowing you to focus 100 percent on your game. Think of relaxation as the key that unlocks the full power of your mindset. Make relaxation a daily habit, both on and off the course, to keep your range finder fully charged and ready to attract success.

Insight Two:
Breathe Consciously

The quickest way to relax, even in the heat of competition, is to take a few deep breaths. This simple act grounds you in the present moment, helping you stay calm, focused, and grateful. Deep breathing is more than just a way to relax—it's a way to reset your mindset, bringing you back to a place of clarity and control. Practice conscious breathing regularly to keep your range finder strong and responsive.

Insight Three:
Understand the Difference
Between Rest and Relaxation

True relaxation is more than just sitting down or watching TV, it's about giving your mind the space to focus and affirm your goals. On the golf course, this means taking the time to mentally prepare before every shot, ensuring that your range finder is aligned with your desired outcome. Make it a priority to find quiet moments during your round to clear your mind and reinforce your focus.

TRUST:
Three Insights to Magnetize Trust in Yourself

Insight One:
Trust the Process

Trust is essential for discovering your true potential. In golf, this means trusting your swing, your decisions, and your ability to handle whatever comes your way. Trust that you have what it takes to succeed, even when you can't see the whole path ahead. This trust will propel you forward, helping you stay committed and confident throughout your game.

Insight Two:
Harness the Power of Words

The words you use, both in your mind and out loud, have a profound impact on your mindset. Positive self-talk can reinforce your trust in yourself and your abilities, while negative talk can undermine your confidence. Choose words that build you up and keep your range finder tuned to success. Speak to yourself as you would to a champion, because that's what you are becoming.

Insight Three:
Recognize That Trust Is Always Evolving

Trusting yourself and your abilities is never static, it's either growing or diminishing. Every round of golf is an opportunity to strengthen your trust in your game. When you commit to building trust, you move closer to your full potential, both on the course and in life. Remember, you're either moving toward your best self or away from it—make sure you're always moving forward.

REPEAT:
Three Insights to Magnetize
Your Resilience

Insight One:
Internal Repetition
Shapes External Results

The thoughts you repeat to yourself shape your reality. If you constantly replay doubts or fears, they will manifest in your game. Instead, focus on constructive thoughts that support your goals. Repeating positive affirmations such as, "I am confident," "I trust my swing," and, "I play with focus" will program your range finder to attract success.

Insight Two:
Repeated Positive Thoughts
Repel Negativity

Consistently repeating constructive thoughts helps repel negative influences and attracts positive energy. This not only benefits you but also those around you—your playing partners, your coaches, and even your competition. A positive mindset is contagious, and by magnetizing your own mindset, you elevate the entire experience of the game.

Insight Three:
Intentional Repetition
Gives You Control

Random positive thoughts are beneficial, but intentionally repeating thoughts that align with your goals is transformative. When you consciously focus on the thoughts that matter most—those directly tied to your success—you take control of your mindset and, by extension, your game. Over time, these intentional thoughts become second nature, helping you stay focused, confident, and unstoppable, no matter what challenges you face.

Solidifying Your Range Finder: A Self-Hypnosis Meditation Exercise

Now let's solidify this concept with a self-hypnosis meditation exercise. If you've been following along with my app's audio programs after each day's reading, you've likely noticed that meditation has been a cornerstone of your daily routine. Have you started to feel more relaxed, calm, and aware? This is no coincidence. By deliberately carving out time for yourself each day, you're making a powerful investment in resetting and rebooting your mind and mental operating system.

Each day has been a step toward mastering the art of mental clarity—emphasizing the critical importance of clearing out the clutter that can cloud your thoughts and derail your focus. Through this process, you've been learning to redirect your mindset with purposeful thoughts and vivid visualization, setting the stage for peak performance both on and off the golf course. The next chapter gives you a self-hypnosis meditation exercise script.

MindsetCaddie Reset

> **Range Finder in Your Mind:** Just as a physical range finder in golf helps you measure distances and make informed decisions on the course, the Range Finder in

Your Mind acts as a mental tool to guide your thoughts, focus, and emotions toward achieving your best outcomes. It's a mental GPS that keeps you aligned with your goals, ensuring that your mindset is always optimized for peak performance.

> **Mastering Relaxation, Trust, and Resilience:** These three principles are essential for strengthening your mental game. Relaxation helps clear your mind and prepare it for high performance; trust allows you to commit fully to your decisions and actions; and repetition builds your resilience to ensure that constructive thoughts and behaviors become ingrained in your mindset, leading to consistent success on the course.

> **Investing Time in You:** The concept of investing in you helps reset, realign, and recharge your mental energy, making it easier to maintain focus, calm, and intentionality, both on and off the golf course. This daily discipline is key to leveraging the power of your range finder in your mind.

Mindsetcaddie Redirect

> Review your "I am" statements, constructive AutoThoughts, and any notes that you have been developing. Make adjustments as needed. This will be used when

customizing your self-hypnosis meditation script in the next chapter.

> As a reinforcement tool, you can now listen to Day Twelve in the audio program in my app. I will guide you through the breathing and meditation exercise to promote calmness, awareness, and guided thought, adding elements based on this chapter.

SELF-HYPNOSIS MEDITATION SCRIPT

Every time we choose action over
excuses, we strengthen our discipline and
move one step closer to our goals.

THIS CHAPTER MARKS a pivotal point in our journey. All the previous chapters and daily practices in this book have served a singular purpose: to reset and redirect your mindset. As you've implemented various exercises and action steps along the way, you've likely experienced the rewards and results of your commitment. Now it's time to implement your customized script with a self-hypnosis meditation exercise that reinforces trust in yourself. The simplicity of this exercise is precisely what makes it so powerful.

By dedicating personal time to focus on your awareness, you can unlock profound outcomes for your mindset and performance. This meditation is not about complex techniques; rather, it's a commitment to quiet minutes when you allow your mind to reset, realign, and recharge. The calm, focused state you achieve stems from your intentional decision to leverage positive intentions, engraving affirmations, suggestions, and guided thoughts into your mindset.

To Begin...

To begin, find a quiet area where you will not be disturbed. Choose a comfortable place to sit, preferably in a chair with armrests, so you can fully relax without worrying about falling over. Alternatively, you can lie down on a bed or a soft surface.

Remember, during this session, you will not be asleep or unconscious but in a deeply relaxed state. If at any time you need to wake up—whether because the phone rings, someone calls your name, or an emergency arises—you will be able to open your eyes and respond immediately. You are always in control; your desire to relax is the only thing guiding you deeper into this state. This is your time, so I recommend that you are alone.

Self-Hypnosis Meditation Induction

Begin by focusing your eyes on a stationary object, either on the wall or the ceiling. Keep your eyes fixed on this object, concentrating as much as you can. Take a deep breath in…and then let the air out slowly, completely relaxing every muscle and bone in your body. Now, count down from three to one, as you do, slowly visualizing your eyes becoming very heavy, like they are made of lead. Allow your eyes to close completely.

> Three: Visualize your eyes becoming heavy, almost as if they're weighted down.

> Two: Your eyes are starting to get watery and blink. They feel so tired now...

> One: Now, completely close your eyes.

Deepening Relaxation

Now, count from one to ten, take deep breaths in and out. With each breath you take in, and each breath you let out, allow yourself to go deeper and deeper into a state of relaxation. Let each exhale send you further into this pleasant, peaceful state.

> *One* (Deep breath in)

> *Two* (Exhale) Let the breath out slowly...

> *Three* (Deep breath in)

> *Four* (Exhale) And relax...

> *Five* (Deep breath in) Feel yourself sinking deeper...

> *Six* (Exhale) Just let yourself go...

> *Seven* (Deep breath in) Heavier and heavier...

> *Eight* (Exhale) Visualize your entire body becoming so heavy, like dead weight or a rag doll...

> *Nine* (Deep breath in)

> *Ten* (Exhale) That's it—way down into a very pleasant form of concentration.

Body Relaxation

Now, begin to relax your entire body, starting from your shoulders and slowly moving all the way down to your toes. Feel the weight of your shoulders releasing, as if a heavy burden is being lifted off. Let this relaxation flow down through your arms... into your hands... as though all the tension is draining away, leaving your arms feeling clear and calm.

As this wave of relaxation continues, feel it moving down your chest... softening your breath and calming your heart. Allow the peaceful sensation to move through your torso, into your waist and hips. Your lower back softens, and any tightness or discomfort fades away.

Next, feel the relaxation spreading to your thighs... knees... and down into your calves. With each breath, your legs grow heavier, completely letting go of any remaining tension. Finally, let the relaxation travel all the way down to your feet and toes. Imagine your toes loosening, your feet sinking gently into the ground, fully relaxed and at ease.

With your entire body now calm and heavy, from your shoulders to your toes, let yourself drift deeper into this state of rest. Each breath you take enhances this relaxation, grounding you even further. You are now completely relaxed, feeling peaceful,

centered, and ready to receive positive and empowering suggestions that will support your mindset growth.

Allow your body to settle even more, feeling completely sup-
ported and at ease, as your mind opens to new possibilities. The
deeper you relax, the more open and receptive you become, and
the more you align with the mindset that will elevate your performance and well-being. Let go completely, knowing you are
exactly where you need to be, fully relaxed from head to toe.

Mindset Awareness

Take a moment to observe the state of mind you're in. You feel
deeply relaxed and at peace. Notice how simple it is to reach this
state—with just a few suggestions and deep breaths, you have
guided your body into a wonderful state of calm.

Now, gently turn your awareness inward, and observe your
thoughts without judgment. You are in control, and you have the
ability to release anything that does not serve you in this moment.
Recognize how your mind, now so clear and calm, has the power
to create this state at any time. Each breath grounds you deeper
into tranquility, and you become aware of the vast potential within
you to reshape your thoughts.

As you continue to examine your mental landscape, appreciate
the simplicity and ease with which you've shifted into this deep
state of relaxation. Let this serve as a reminder that, at any time,
you can return to this place of inner calm and clarity and use it as
a foundation to build the mindset you desire.

Positive Suggestions

You are now ready to absorb positive suggestions and visualizations that will enhance your mindset. Allow what resonates with you to sink deeply into your subconscious. Feel your body relax even further. Visualize yourself as strong, confident, and in control. You now know how to handle yourself better in stressful situations. If you ever start to feel uncomfortable or notice a buildup of unwanted tension, simply PAUSE and take a deep, deep breath, then release it. You will feel calm and in control, no matter the situation.

Insert Your Personal Script

At this point, visualize your personal script, much like a grocery list written clearly in your mind. This is your new software update. Remember you are the programmer of your internal operating system of your mindset. Use the "I am" statements, constructive AutoThoughts, visualizations, and the notes that you have developed. You can even say to yourself your unique "trigger word" to reset and redirect your mindset. This is your time to shift your perspective and ignite your talent. See it laid out in front of you, with each item representing a specific intention, goal, or affirmation that supports your growth and success!

As you mentally review your updated software code, take your time with each item. Picture it vividly, as though you're picking each item off the shelf and placing it into your cart of personal transformation. For example, the first item might be **unshakable focus**—imagine selecting focus and placing it into your mental basket. See yourself standing on the tee box, completely locked in, fully present for each shot, without distraction.

Next on the list might be **patience and resilience**—imagine grabbing resilience, seeing yourself in a situation where the shot didn't go as planned, yet you're composed, focused, and ready for the next one. You no longer dwell on past mistakes; instead, you respond with calm and renewed determination.

As you continue down the list, select **confidence under pressure**—see yourself standing over a critical putt. In this relaxed state, visualize your body and mind in perfect harmony, feeling that confidence flowing through you as you approach the ball with precision and trust. You know you have prepared for this moment, so you embrace it with full confidence in your abilities.

Perhaps your next item is **clarity of mind**—imagine the clutter of doubts, fears, and distractions being swept away like leaves in the wind. Visualize your mind as clear as a sunny fairway, guiding you with precision through each swing, each decision, free of overthinking. With this clarity, you play the course with ease, trusting your instincts.

Another item on your script could be **mental toughness**—picture yourself remaining composed when challenges arise, whether it's a tough lie in the rough or an unexpected obstacle. Visualize yourself making strategic decisions, staying in control, and using your mental strength to turn challenges into opportunities for growth.

As you review each item—*focus, resilience, confidence, clarity, mental toughness*—affirm their presence in your game and your life. Say to yourself, "I am focused and have clarity on the course. I am confident in every swing. I am resilient and patient with every shot." These affirmations are tools that will guide you not just through a round of golf, but through any challenge you face.

Regardless of your personal script, this is the time to fully embrace your new software. Just as you update a program for improved performance, this is your moment to update your mindset. Picture your mind like a computer being reprogrammed with new, positive intentions. You are installing the mental software that aligns with your highest potential.

Let go of any outdated patterns or limiting beliefs that may have held you back. As you embrace this update, feel the shift happening within you, as though a fresh wave of energy is flowing through your mind, ready to take action on the positive intentions you've set. This new mindset software is designed for success, resilience, and focus. Every time you step onto the golf course—or face any challenge in life—this software will activate, guiding you with clarity, confidence, and purpose.

Feel how clear and powerful your mind is now, ready to act on these intentions effortlessly. Trust that this mental update is deeply embedded within you, ready to shape your thoughts, actions, and outcomes from this moment forward. This mindset will lead you to perform at your best, no matter the circumstances.

Opening Your Eyes

As this exercise comes to a close, take a few more deep breaths. When you are ready and you feel your time has been well spent engraving your personal script, gently bring your awareness back to the present moment. Wiggle your fingers and toes, and when you feel fully ready, slowly open your eyes, feeling refreshed, confident, and ready to take on whatever challenges come your way. *Now open your eyes! Eyes Open!*

I share this exercise with you as a flexible tool that can be molded and shaped to best fit your personal needs. You can tailor this experience to suit your preferences and deepen your practice over time. To further enhance this exercise, I invite you to listen to the Day Thirteen audio track in my app, which will guide you even more deeply into the process.

MindsetCaddie Reset

> **Review Your Script:** Make any adjustments or additions needed to your personal script. Remember, your script is your personal software update, and it can change daily based on your needs and intensions.

> **Take Action:** Taking the time to implement this self-hypnosis meditation exercise with your personal script, empowers your inner mindset coach, helping you build mental clarity, enhance focus, and strengthen your resilience under pressure. By consistently practicing this exercise, you train your mind to automatically align with positive thoughts and actions, allowing you to approach challenges with confidence and a calm, focused mindset. This powerful tool not only improves your performance on the golf course but also in all areas of life, as it reinforces your ability to stay grounded and achieve your best outcomes.

MindsetCaddie Redirect

> As a reinforcement tool, you can now listen to Day Thirteen in the audio program in my app. I will guide you through the breathing and meditation exercise to promote calmness, awareness, and guided thought, adding your personal script

19TH HOLE REFLECTION

Through reflection, we uncover lessons that strengthen our resilience and shape our future.

I DISTINCTLY REMEMBER the moment when the concept of the *19th Hole Reflection* first took shape in my mind. It was many years ago, and I was having lunch with a client at a golf club after a round. We were seated in the clubhouse, enjoying our meal and discussing the day's events. The atmosphere was lively, with groups of golfers unwinding after their rounds, sharing stories, and laughing together.

As we talked, I couldn't help but overhear a conversation at a nearby table. A group of guys were having drinks and talking about their game. It was a familiar scene—friends catching up, ribbing each other, and reliving the highs and lows of their rounds. But one man in the group stood out to me. He was the outspoken one, always talking, always joking, and always had an opinion. At first, it seemed like harmless banter—typical post-round chatter that is often heard among golfers. But as the conversation contin-ued, something struck a chord with me.

This man's comments weren't just playful jabs; they were laced with a heavy dose of self-criticism. He joked about his poor shots, belittled his own performance, and seemed to take a perverse pleasure in pointing out his mistakes and those of his friends. What really caught my attention was how self-destructive this dialogue felt. It was as if he was using humor as a shield to mask deeper frustrations and insecurities about his game.

I couldn't stop thinking about how this kind of talk, even when disguised as friendly joking, could be detrimental if taken too far. Now I'm not saying that friendly joking isn't a good thing—on the contrary, it's a big part of the camaraderie that makes golf enjoy-able. But when self-critical banter becomes excessive, it can start to take a toll, not just on your mood, but on your confidence and performance as well.

"Perpetuating negative self-talk may carry over into future rounds.

As I continued my lunch, the idea of the 19th Hole Reflection began to take shape in my mind. I realized how powerful those post-round conversations could be—not just in reinforcing posi-tive aspects of the game, but also in perpetuating negative self-talk that could carry over into future rounds. The 19th hole, often associ-ated with relaxation and socializing, was also a critical juncture for mental reflection. How you talk about your game in these moments could set the tone for how you approach your next round.

Internal Reflection

The internal dialogue is where most of the post-round process-ing occurs. Many golfers replay the round in their minds, shot by shot, thinking about what they could have done better. This self-assessment is crucial for growth and improvement, but it often comes with a downside—negative self-talk.

When you focus on the missed shots, the putts that lipped out, or the drives that veered off course, it's easy to spiral into self-crit-icism. This negative self-talk tends to dominate, taking up more space and time in your mind. You might catch yourself saying, "I should have made that putt," or "Why did I hit that shot so poorly?" These thoughts can be hard to shake, and if left unchecked, they can chip away at your confidence and enjoyment of the game.

Positive Reflection

On the flip side, there are moments when you reflect on the round with a sense of pride and self-appreciation. Perhaps you made an amazing shot or managed a difficult hole exceptionally well. These are the moments that should be celebrated and reinforced in your mind. However, they often get overshadowed by the more critical, negative reflections.

Balancing the Reflection

The goal of this chapter is to help you find balance in your post-round reflection. While it's important to learn from mistakes, it's equally crucial to acknowledge your successes. After all, reflection isn't just about identifying what went wrong, it's also about recognizing what went right.

One technique to achieve this balance is to consciously direct your internal dialogue. After a round, take a moment to mentally review your performance, but with a structured approach:

1. *Start with the Positives:* Begin by acknowledging the things you did well. Identify at least three positive aspects of your game—these could be great shots, smart decisions, or moments of focus and resilience.

2. *Constructive Criticism:* When you think about the areas that need improvement, frame them in a constructive way. Instead of saying, "I messed up that drive," say, "Next time, I'll focus more on my setup to improve my drive."

3. **Set Intentions:** Use your reflection to set intentions for your next round. What will you do differently? What will you continue to do well? Setting these intentions can help shift your mindset from one of criticism to one of growth and opportunity.

4. **Express Gratitude:** Finally, end your reflection with gratitude. Be thankful for the opportunity to play, for the moments of joy the game brings, and for the lessons learned.

19th Hole Reflection

After your next round and you head to the clubhouse, this is where the 19th Hole Reflection comes into play. The 19th hole is not just a place to relax and socialize, it's also an opportunity to reflect on your round in a social setting. If you played well, these conversations can be filled with pride and shared stories of great shots and successful strategies. However, if the round didn't go as planned, the conversations often turn to what went wrong.

Fill your conversations with pride and stories of great shots and successful strategies.

When we've played poorly, the discussion at the 19th hole often revolves around missed opportunities, frustrations, and the mistakes that were made. While it's natural to want to vent or commiserate with others, these conversations can sometimes reinforce the negative self-talk that began during your internal reflection. Dwelling on the negatives with others can make them feel even more significant, further diminishing your confidence and enjoyment.

Shaping the Conversation

Just as you guide your internal reflection, it's important to shape your 19th hole reflections in a way that's constructive. Share your successes, discuss what you learned, and be mindful of how you talk about the areas where you struggled. Encourage your friends to do the same. By focusing on growth and improvement, even in a social setting, you can create a more positive and supportive environment that benefits everyone.

How you perceive yourself in these 19th hole reflections can significantly influence how you approach your next round. If you allow the negative aspects of your game to dominate the conversation, it can cement a sense of inadequacy or doubt in your mind. This mindset can carry over into your next round, setting you up for a repeat of the same mistakes. On the other hand, if you focus on your strengths and what you did well, you reinforce a positive self-image. This positive reinforcement can build your confidence and set the stage for a more successful and enjoyable round the next time you play.

The Impact of Perception on Future Performance

The way you talk about your game at the 19th hole is not just about sharing your experiences—it's about reinforcing your self-perception. If you constantly criticize yourself in front of others, you start to believe those criticisms on a deeper level. This can create a self-fulfilling prophecy where your negative expectations become reality in your future games.

Conversely, by discussing your game in a balanced way— acknowledging both the good and the areas for improvement—you set a tone of growth and resilience. This approach helps to create a mental environment where you're more likely to perform well in your next round. When you reflect on your game socially, make a conscious effort to highlight what you did well and frame your challenges as opportunities for improvement.

Balanced reflection enhances your mindset and prepares you for better future performance.

By consciously guiding both your internal and 19th hole reflections, you can prevent negative self-talk from dominating your thoughts and instead create a balanced, constructive post-round review. This balanced reflection not only enhances your mindset but also prepares you for better performance in future rounds. So next time you finish a round, whether you're reflecting alone or with friends at the 19th hole, remember: how you reflect on your game can be as important as how you play it. Choose to reflect in a way that supports your growth, confidence, and enjoyment of the game. By doing so, you set yourself up for continued success, not only in your next round but in your overall approach to the game.

Mindsetcaddie Reset

> **Balance Your Reflection:** After a round of golf, it's important to balance your reflection by acknowledging both your successes and areas for improvement. This approach prevents negative self-talk from dominating your thoughts and helps maintain a constructive mindset that fuels growth and confidence.

> **Shape Your Social Reflections:** The conversations you have at the 19th hole are more than just casual chatter—they shape your self-perception and influence your future performance. By guiding these discussions

to focus on positive aspects and learning opportunities, you reinforce a mindset of resilience and optimism.

> **Perception Influences Performance:** How you perceive and talk about your game, both internally and externally, can set the tone for your next round. A positive, growth-oriented reflection can enhance your confidence and prepare you for better outcomes, while excessive self-criticism can lead to repeated mistakes and diminished enjoyment of the game.

MindsetCaddie Redirect

> Pause before you reflect and set the tone of your internal and external conversation.

- Identify three positives from your round.
- Frame criticisms constructively.
- Set clear intentions for your next round.
- Guide your 19th hole conversations to focus on growth and improvement.
- End with gratitude.

> As a reinforcement tool, you can now listen to Day Fourteen in the audio program in my app.

SELF-REGULATION

Growth is not measured by how far you've come,
but by how much you've learned along the way.

BEFORE YOU EMBARKED on this 14-day journey to enhance your golf mindset, your thoughts and beliefs were already shaping your game, your outcomes, and your life. Whether you realized it or not, your mindset was guiding your every move on the course, dictating how you approached each shot, how you handled pressure, and ultimately, how you performed. The only difference now is that you've become aware of this process—and that awareness has given you the power to take control.

As you reflect on the lessons you've learned over these past 14 days, remember that this journey doesn't end here. The real secret to transforming your golf game and your life lies in the continuation of these practices. You've started something powerful, but the key to lasting change is to keep the momentum going.

The Power of Awareness in Your Game

The minute you became aware that you wanted to enhance your golf skills, you set the wheels in motion. Your awareness of what you aspire to achieve—whether it's lowering your handicap, mastering your swing, or improving your mental game—has been the driving force behind your progress. By simply recognizing what you want to accomplish, you've already begun to make it a reality. This awareness is your most powerful tool, and it's something you need to carry with you every day, on and off the course.

Accountability Drives Your Game

There are countless variables beyond your control—wind, course conditions, weather, or even a bad bounce. These factors can easily derail your round if you let them. However, there is one constant that can elevate your game to the next level—accountability.

Accountability means taking full ownership of your actions, decisions, and mindset on the course. You cannot control external factors, but you can control how you respond to them. Your reaction to adversity shapes the outcome of your game. Whether you're redirecting from a poor shot or staying focused through distractions, accountability is what transforms challenges into opportunities for growth.

The *Accountability Mindset* in golf is about stepping up and owning every shot you take. No excuses. Instead of blaming external conditions or past mistakes, you control the chain reaction that leads to a better, more focused round. Embracing accountability pushes you to take responsibility for your actions, learn from setbacks, and cultivate a mindset that drives constant improvement.

Accountability is the guiding force that helps you navigate the unpredictable nature of golf. It's what separates great golfers from good ones—champions hold themselves accountable, knowing that every decision, every swing, and every mental approach is theirs to own. By adopting accountability as a core principle, you empower yourself to stay focused, bounce back from tough moments, and move forward with determination toward your goals.

When you make accountability the foundation of your game, you shift from being a passive participant to an active driver of your performance. Accountability means responding with intention rather than reacting emotionally. It leads to sharper focus, stronger execution, and a mindset that allows you to overcome obstacles and push through frustration.

Accountability fosters confidence and authenticity in your approach to the game.

As you commit to accountability, you build trust—not only within yourself but with those around you. Accountability fosters confidence and authenticity in your approach to the game. Golf often throws unexpected challenges your way, but by adopting an *accountability mindset,* you create an anchor of stability. It helps you stay grounded, respond thoughtfully, and keep progressing toward your aspirations with renewed focus and purpose.

Remember, while many things in golf are beyond your control, accountability is not. By fully embracing accountability, you become the architect of your success. It allows you to shape your own growth, transform challenges into opportunities, and become a powerful catalyst for positive change on the course. Accountability is the key to unlocking your best game—own it!

The Journey Continues

This journey of lessons learned to leverage your mindset is much like your golf game—it requires consistent attention, practice, and repetition to see the maximum benefit. The more you focus on it, the more powerful it becomes. The mindset techniques you've learned over the past 14 days are tools you should continue to use and refine. This process has been working in your life, whether you were conscious of it or not; but now, you're in control. You have the power to direct your mindset, and with that power comes the responsibility to keep moving forward.

Just like on the golf course, where improvement happens over time through dedication, persistence, and thoughtful reflection, your mindset will continue to evolve. The more you practice these techniques, the more automatic and effective they become, allowing you to respond to challenges with greater ease and confidence. Every shot you take is an opportunity to reinforce what you've learned—whether it's staying calm under pressure, maintaining focus, or bouncing back from setbacks.

The real journey begins after the initial foundation has been laid. This is where the work deepens. As you continue to apply these principles, you will begin to notice more subtle shifts in your thinking, your reactions, and your overall performance, both on and off the course. *Consistency is key.* It's not about perfection, but about continually making progress, learning from every experience, and adjusting along the way.

Understand that growth is not always linear—there will be ups and downs. Some days everything will click, and other days you may struggle. But this is all part of the process. Stay committed. Every challenge is an opportunity for growth. Embrace the setbacks as they teach you resilience, persistence, and adaptability. Keep showing up, keep practicing, and remember that mastery comes with time.

Embrace setbacks—each teaches you resilience, persistence, and adaptability. Keep showing up, keep practicing— mastery comes with time.

The journey doesn't end here—it's ongoing, and it's yours to shape. Keep pushing forward, and remember: the more you invest in your mindset, the more it will reward you in ways you may not yet even realize. Now that you hold the tools in your hands, it's up to you to decide how you will use them. The journey ahead is full of potential and possibility, and with a mindset rooted in accountability and growth, there are no limits to what you can achieve. Keep driving forward—your best is yet to come.

Reflect and Refine

As you continue on this journey, take time to reflect on what resonated most with you during these 14 days. What lessons made the biggest impact? Which exercises helped you the most? Reflection is essential—it allows you to gain insight into your progress, identify areas where you're thriving, and highlight any adjustments that could deepen your practice. By actively engaging in this self-reflection, you reinforce the positive changes and keep your focus on growth.

The beauty of this personal awareness plan and accompanying audio program is that it's not a one-time experience—you can repeat it, revisit specific chapters/days, listen to the audio, and continue to refine your mindset. Just as you wouldn't expect to master a golf swing in one lesson, mastering your mindset requires repetition. Every time you engage with these practices, they become more ingrained, strengthening your mental game and making it feel more natural to apply these techniques under pressure. With every reflection and every moment of refinement, you sharpen your edge.

Stay Flexible

While consistency is key, flexibility is also important. There will be days when life gets busy or things don't go as planned, and that's okay. The goal isn't to be perfect but to be adaptable. If you miss a day or two, don't beat yourself up—simply get back on track. The strength of your mindset lies in your ability to adjust and keep moving forward. Flexibility is not a sign of weakness, it's a sign of resilience. Staying committed, even when life throws you a curveball, is how you maintain long-term momentum.

Celebrate Your Growth

Remember to celebrate your progress. Every step forward, no matter how small, is a victory. Acknowledge your growth and the positive shifts you've experienced, both on the golf course and in your personal life. Celebrate the fact that you have taken control of your mindset, and that you are continuously refining it to become the best version of yourself. This journey is about progress, not perfection, and every moment you invest in yourself is a step toward reaching your full potential.

Keep this momentum alive, and you will find that not only will your golf game improve, your mindset will transform in ways that positively affect every area of your life. You have the tools, the discipline, and the mindset to continue growing—now it's time to see where this journey takes you.

Reinforce Your Commitment

To deepen your awareness and commitment, I invite you to ask yourself these questions regularly, using your phone, a notebook, or a document on your computer:

> What do I really want to achieve in my golf game?

> How will I know when I've reached this goal? What will it look, sound, and feel like?

> ❯ What is my time frame for accomplishing this? What is my plan?

Spend at least five minutes writing out your thoughts. This exercise is critical for reinforcing your goals and keeping your mindset focused on what you want to achieve. Clarity leads to action, and action leads to results.

The Real Secret: Keep Moving Forward

The real secret to success in both golf and life is to keep moving forward. Your mindset has always been working behind the scenes, but now that you're aware of its power, you can direct it more effectively. Remember, this is a lifelong journey. The more you practice, the more your constructive thoughts and beliefs will replace the old, destructive ones. It's up to you to nurture these new thoughts, day by day, until they become second nature.

To maintain this momentum, I encourage you to dedicate time every day to continue this work. Make it a priority in your schedule—a personal appointment with yourself, even if it's just 10 minutes a day. The important thing is not necessarily when you do it, but that you consistently show up for yourself. This small, daily commitment will lead to monumental transformations in both your game and your life.

This daily practice is more than just a habit—it's an investment in your future success. Think of it as your mental warm-up, just like you prepare your body before a round of golf. A few minutes of focused attention can set the tone for your day, keeping you grounded, clear-minded, and ready to tackle challenges with confidence. Over time, this consistency builds momentum, and what begins as a simple 10-minute routine can evolve into a mindset that positively impacts every aspect of your life.

Now, as we reach the conclusion of this journey together, I want to remind you that this is just the beginning. Throughout this book, I've been your mindset coach, guiding you through the steps to harness the power of your mind. But now, it's your turn. The real transformation happens when you take ownership of this process and make it a continual practice in your life.

I encourage you to keep utilizing the programs available in my app—they're designed to support you as you move forward. When I wrote *Leverage Your Mindset*, my first book, I had a hidden agenda: I wanted to spark self-discovery. What I found through working with truly successful people is that they didn't just read the book once—they returned to it again and again. They made notes, revisited key concepts, and refined their approach as they evolved.

Now, I'm not saying you're wrong if you didn't make notes. But if you've found value in this process, I encourage you to repeat it as much as you like. Each time you go through the material, you'll uncover new insights; and as successful people do, write some notes in the margins or highlight portions that hit home. If I had started this book by telling you to read it multiple times, you might have thought, *I'm not committing to that*. But now, after seeing the results and the power of these techniques, you're likely more engaged and you understand that the coaching never truly stops.

This is not about a one-time fix; it's about creating a lifelong practice of growth, learning, and refinement. Every time you revisit these lessons, you unlock more of your potential, both on the golf course and in life. So keep moving forward, stay committed to your journey, and remember—you have the power to shape your future through the strength of your mindset. This is just the beginning, and you will be amazed at where your journey takes you.

MindsetCaddie Reset

> **Believe it and You Will See it**: Your mindset is always aligning your outcomes with your deepest beliefs. If you believe success is possible, your mindset will work to prove you right. Feed your mind with positive, constructive thoughts, and watch as your mindset magnetizes you toward your goals.

> **Self-Discovery Never Ends**: *Leverage Your Mindset for Golfers* is your key to unlocking and maximizing your daily potential. Knowing what you want is the first step. Hold yourself accountable, and take consistent action toward your goals every day. Awareness combined with action creates results. This process is continuous, guiding you on the daily journey to becoming the best

version of yourself. This 14-day plan is just the beginning. The more you integrate these practices into your daily routine, the more they will become second nature. Make it a habit, and you will see monumental changes in your game and in every aspect of your life.

MindsetCaddie Redirect

> Use your relaxation and meditation exercises to continually update your mindset. Keep refining and reinforcing the thoughts and beliefs that align with your goals. Schedule time every day for an additional 14 days, and repeat the process regularly to ensure your mindset remains your greatest asset.

> As a reinforcement tool, you can now access the final audio program in my app for this book, titled *SELF REGULATION*. This track is designed to support your ongoing journey and help you stay on track to achieving your goals.

> Make *Leveraging Your Mindset* part of your daily operating plan. Even if it was just one simple example, concept, or redirect, be accountable. Choose to enjoy the game you love.

THANK YOU

AS YOU HAVE reached the final pages of this book, I want to take a moment to thank you for joining me on this journey. Whether you're a seasoned golfer or just beginning to explore the mental side of the game, your willingness to dive deeper into your mindset is truly commendable.

Golf is as much about the mind as it is about the swing, and I hope the strategies and insights shared on the previous pages have sparked something within you—a new way of thinking, approaching the game, and ultimately, life itself.

The tools and techniques you've learned on the golf course aren't just for improving your game, they can profoundly influence every area of your personal and professional life. The mindset you cultivate—focus, resilience, and adaptability—empowers you to succeed in business, strengthen relationships, and become a better version of yourself daily. As I travel the world, speaking to sales teams, leaders, entrepreneurs, and organizations, it's incredibly rewarding to witness how these principles transform not only performance but also how people approach challenges and embrace growth.

The fact that you committed your time and attention to this process means you are already on the path to greater success. Remember, this journey is ongoing, and your mindset will continue to evolve and serve you, not only on the course but in everything you do.

Thank you for allowing me to be part of your journey. Here's to your continued growth, your future achievements, and your unwavering belief in your own potential.

Mindset Matters,

RICKY KALMON

Visionary Architect in Personal Growth

RICKY KALMON is a mindset expert, motivational speaker, and celebrity hypnotist who delivers high-energy and motivational keynote programs. His programs are inspirational and offer compelling, applicable tools anyone can use in personal and professional development. Kalmon reveals how our mindset can be the greatest tool in achieving new heights, reducing stress, and increasing productivity and potential.

Ricky Kalmon's mindset message and techniques will change the way you live, work, and think. Kalmon works with Fortune 500 companies, sales teams, leaders, executives, and sports teams, teaching them how to reinforce their thoughts and beliefs to enhance their results. By creating awareness of your thoughts, Kalmon reveals how to enhance your mindset to eliminate doubt and ignite your positive intentions. Through his programs, thousands have changed their world by changing the way they think.

Benefits of Ricky Kalmon's programs include:

> Stress reduction / mindfulness / sales growth mindset
> Overcome challenges / adapt to change
> Enhance accountability and potential
> Reinforce confidence and belief
> Ignite purpose and prosperity

As an international speaker, motivator, and success expert, Ricky will take you and your organization to the next level of success.

For more information visit:
www.rickykalmon.com

NOTES

Use these blank pages as your
personal notes page.

NOTES

NOTES

SOURCES AND ADDITIONAL REFERENCES

Crystal Raypole, "Yes, Self-Hypnosis Can Really Work—Here's How to Give It a Try," *healthline.com,* August 17, 2021; https://www .healthline.com/health/mental-health/self-hypnosis; accessed November 22, 2024.

Zephyr Melton, "Can you hypnotize yourself into playing better golf? Expert explains," *Golf.com,* June 7, 2024; https://golf.com/ instruction/hypnotize-into-better-golf-play-smart/; accessed November 22, 2024.

Sara Reistad-Long, "Positive Thinking Sets You Up for Success," *WebMD,* http://www.webmd.com/balance/features/power -positive-thinking#1; accessed November 22, 2024.

Barbara L. Fredrickson, "The broaden-and-build theory of positive emotions," *Philosophical Transactions of the Royal Society* B 359, no. 1449 (September 29, 2004): 1367-1378; http://www.ncbi .nlm.nih.gov/pmc/articles/PMC1693418/pdf/15347528.pdf.

W. Staffen, et al., "Selective brain activity in response to one's own name in the persistent vegetative state," *Journal of Neurology, Neurosurgery & Psychiatry* 77(12) (December 2006), 1383-1384; http://www.ncbi.nlm.nih.gov/pmc/articles/PMC2077408/#; accessed November 22, 2024.

Joel Wong and Joshua A. Brown, "How Gratitude Changes You and Your Brain," *Greater Good Magazine*, June 6, 2017, http://greatergood.berkeley.edu/article/item/how_gratitude_changes _you_and_your_brain; accessed November 22, 2024.

Sarah Gardner and Dave Albee, "Study focuses on strategies for achieving goals, resolutions," *Dominican University of California*, 2015; https://scholar.dominican.edu/cgi/viewcontent.cgi?article=1265&context=news-releases; accessed November 22, 2024.

Sonja Lyubomirsky, Laura King, and Ed Diener, "The benefits of frequent positive affect: does happiness lead to success?" *Psychological Bulletin* 131, no. 6 (2005), 803-855; https://pubmed.ncbi.nlm.nih.gov/16351326/; accessed November 22, 2024.

Gail Matthews, "The Impact of Commitment, Accountability, and Written Goals on Goal Achievement" (2007), Psychology, Faculty Presentations, 3; https://scholar.dominican.edu/psychology-faculty-conference-presentations/3; accessed November 22, 2024.

Bryan Borzykowski, "Why talking to yourself is the first sign of success," *BBC.com*, April 27, 2017; http://www.bbc.com/worklife/article/20170428-why-talking-to-yourself-is-the-first -sign-of-success; accessed November 22, 2024.

Mary Brabeck, Jill Jeffrey, and Sara Fry, "Practice for Knowledge Acquisition (Not Drill and Kill)," *American Psychological Association*, 2010; http://www.apa.org/education/k12/practice -acquisition; accessed November 22, 2024.

Keith A. Kaufman, Carol R. Glass, and Diane B. Arnkoff, "Evaluation of Mindful Sport Performance Enhancement (MSPE): A New Approach to Promote Flow in Athletes," *Journal of Clinical Sport Psychology* 4 (2009), 334-356; https:// www.thetrueathleteproject.org/uploads/3/1/3/9/31399101/ jcsp_mspe_for_flow_1.pdf; accessed November 22, 2024.

Leonard Reinecke and Wilhelm Hofmann, "Slacking Off or Winding Down? An Experience Sampling Study on the Drivers and Consequences of Media Use for Recovery Versus Procrastination," *Human Communication Research* 42, no. 3 (2016): 441-461.

Therese J. Bouchard, "Words Can Change Your Brain," *Psych Central*, last modified May 27, 2019, https://thereseborchard .com/words-can-change-your-brain/; accessed November 22, 2024.

"You Get What You Pay For? Costly Placebo Works Better Than Cheaper One," *ScienceDaily*, March 5, 2008, http://www .sciencedaily.com/releases/2008/03/080304173339.htm; accessed November 22, 2024.

"Hypnosis for Health—Can Trances Work?" *NIH News in Health*, July 2019, https://newsinhealth.nih.gov/2019/07/hypnosis -health; accessed November 22, 2024.

"Relaxation Techniques: What You Need to Know," *National Center for Complementary and Integrative Health*, June 2021; https://

www.nccih.nih.gov/health/relaxation-techniques-what-you
-need-to-know; accessed November 22, 2024.

Jack Milko, "Bryson DeChambeau goes viral for hysterical 3-putt
sign, offers advice for amateur golfers," *SB Nation's Playing
Through,* November 4, 2024; https://www.sbnation.com/
golf/2024/11/4/24287877/bryson-dechambeau-viral-putting
-advice-amateur-golfers; accessed November 22, 2024.

The secret to turning your best intentions into your greatest accomplishments is here.

LEVERAGE YOUR MINDSET

Overcome Limiting Beliefs and Amplify Your Life!
Be Less Stressed, Happier, and More Mindful!